TERRORISM, HOT SPOTS AND CONFLICT-RELATED ISSUES

THE COST OF WAR AND TERROR OPERATIONS SINCE 9-11

TERRORISM, HOT SPOTS AND CONFLICT-RELATED ISSUES

Additional books in this series can be found on Nova's website under the Series tab.

Additional e-books in this series can be found on Nova's website under the e-book tab.

TERRORISM, HOT SPOTS AND CONFLICT-RELATED ISSUES

THE COST OF WAR AND TERROR OPERATIONS SINCE 9-11

JAMIE VALDEZ
EDITOR

nova publishers
New York

Library of Congress Cataloging-in-Publication Data

ISBN: 978-1-63482-935-9

Published by Nova Science Publishers, Inc. † New York

CONTENTS

Preface

With enactment of the FY2014 Consolidated Appropriations Act on January 1, 2014, Congress has approved appropriations for the past 13 years of war that total $1.6 trillion for military operations, base support, weapons maintenance, training of Afghan and Iraq security forces, reconstruction, foreign aid, embassy costs, and veterans' health care for the war operations initiated since the 9/11 attacks. This book discusses the cost of Iraq, Afghanistan, and other global war of terror operations since 9/11 in detail, and provides information on the FY2015 funding to counter Ebola and the Islamic State (IS).

In: The Cost of War …
Editor: Jamie Valdez
ISBN: 978-1-63482-935-9

Chapter 1

THE COST OF IRAQ, AFGHANISTAN, AND OTHER GLOBAL WAR ON TERROR OPERATIONS SINCE 9/11*

Amy Belasco

SUMMARY

With enactment of the FY2014 Consolidated Appropriations Act on January 1, 2014 (H.R. 3547/P.L. 113-73), Congress has approved appropriations for the past 13 years of war that total $1.6 trillion for military operations, base support, weapons maintenance, training of Afghan and Iraq security forces, reconstruction, foreign aid, embassy costs, and veterans' health care for the war operations initiated since the 9/11 attacks.

Of this $1.6 trillion total, CRS estimates that the total is distributed as follows:

- $686 billion (43%) for Operation Enduring Freedom (OEF) for Afghanistan and other counterterror operations received;
- $815 billion (51%) for Operation Iraqi Freedom (OIF)/Operation New Dawn (OND);

* This is an edited, reformatted and augmented version of a Congressional Research Service publication RL33110, prepared for Members and Committees of Congress dated December 8, 2014.

- $27 billion (2%) for Operation Noble Eagle (ONE), providing enhanced security at military bases; and
- $81 billion (5%) for war-designated funding not considered directly related to the Afghanistan or Iraq wars.

About 92% of the funds are for Department of Defense (DOD), 6% for State Department foreign aid programs and diplomatic operations, 1% for Department of Veterans Administration's medical care for veterans. In addition, 5% of the funds (across agencies) are for programs and activities tangentially-related to war operations.

The FY2015 war request for DOD, State/USAID, and Veterans Administration Medical totals $73.5 billion including $58.1 billion for Afghanistan, $5.0 billion for Iraq, $ 100 million for enhanced security, and $10.4 billion for other war-designated funding. These totals do not reflect the new FY2015 request submitted in November 2014 to cover expenses for Operations Inherent Resolve (OIR) that began with airstrikes launched in late August 2014, to aid Syrian insurgents and the Iraq government to counter the takeover of territory by the Islamic State (IS). The Administration submitted a $5.5 billion FY2015 budget amendment for this operation that Congress is considering. Including the new request, the FY2015 war funding now totals $79.0 billion.

In late May 2014, the President announced that troop levels in Afghanistan would fall from 33,000 to 9,800 by January 1, 2015 with the U.S. role focusing on advising Afghan security forces and conducting counter-terror operations. A year later, by January 1, 2016, the President stated that the number of troops in Afghanistan would halve to about 4,900 and then by the beginning of 2017, settle at an embassy presence of about 1,000.

Overall U.S. troop levels in Afghanistan and Iraq began to decline with the withdrawal of all U.S. troops from Iraq by December 2011. The troop decline continued with President Obama's announcement in February 2013 that the number of U.S. troops in Afghanistan would halve from 67,000 to 34,000 by February 2014. Annual war costs also decreased from a peak of $195 billion in FY2008 to $95 billion enacted in FY2014. After the reversal of the 2009 Afghanistan surge, the President promised in the 2013 State of the Union address that "our troops will continue coming home at a steady pace as Afghan security forces move into the lead [and] our mission will change from combat to support." He also stated that by "2014, this process of transition will be complete, and the Afghan people will be responsible for their own security."

The FY2015 Continuing Resolution (H.J.Res. 124/P.L. 113-164) sets war funding at the FY2014 enacted level of $95.5 billion, which exceeds the FY2015 amended request (with OIR) by about $16.5 billion. The CR expires on December 11, 2014, and Congress is expected to enact another CR or an Omnibus appropriations act for the rest of the fiscal year.

Congress may face several budgetary issues about how to respond to the FY2015 war request and longer-term war cost issues including:

- assessing the amount, purposes, and level of funding to support U.S. troops during the post-2014 drawdown;
- evaluating the Administration proposal for a new flexible funding account that would provide $5 billion for a Counterterrorism Partnerships Fund (CTFP) to respond to unspecified "evolving threats from South Asia to the Sahel" by "building partnership capacity" through Train & Equip programs;
- defining what is an appropriate war-related cost as opposed to what is in the base, non-war budget, a choice made more difficult in part by the potential squeeze on agencies' base budgets that are subject to Budget Control Act spending limits (P.L. 112-25);
- estimating the potential long-term cost of the war, including repairing and replacing war-worn equipment and maintaining an "enduring presence" that could entail a substantial footprint in the region; and
- responding to the November 2014 request for $5.5 billion for Operation Inherent Resolve, the new operation to counter the Islamic State.

There are some indications that the FY2015 DOD war funding request may be more than is needed in light of FY2014 experience when expenses for returning troops and equipment have proven to be lower and the pace faster than anticipated. If expenses are lower and withdrawal is faster than anticipated, the FY2015 request may also include excess funds that could be used to pay for part or all of the new $5.5 billion request to counter the Islamic State. Savings in FY2015 could be partly offset by the recent announcement by Secretary Hagel that up to 1,000 U.S. troops could be kept in Afghanistan until the spring of 2015 to substitute for a delay in NATO troops being available to provide needed support.

Members have raised various concerns about the broad authorities requested for the new CTPF, which exceed current authorities for other Train & Equip programs. The conference version of the FY2015 National Defense

Authorization Act, H.R. 3797, reduces the funding and rejects most of the new authorities requested. Other concerns include the lack of evidence of success in previous similar programs, particularly in situations like the complex political-military environment in Syria and Iraq.

Congress may wish to consider ways to restrict war-funding to exclude activities marginally related to war operations and support, and to limit the use of ground troops in Operation Inherent Resolve.

INTRODUCTION

Since the terrorist attacks of September 11, 2001, the U.S. Armed Forces, under guidance from the Department of Defense (DOD), have conducted the following military operations:

- Operation Enduring Freedom (OEF) in Afghanistan and other small Global War on Terror (GWOT) operations like the Philippines and Djibouti that began immediately after the 9/11 attacks and continue;
- Operation Iraqi Freedom (OIF) that began in the fall of 2002 with the buildup of troops for the March 2003 invasion of Iraq and continued with counter-insurgency and stability operations until 2010;
- Operation New Dawn (OND), a successor to OIF that began on September 1, 2010, when U.S. troops adopted an advisory and assistance role and concluded in December 2011 when all U.S. troops withdrew from Iraq (though some 13,000 combat-ready troops remain in Kuwait);
- Operation Noble Eagle (ONE) providing enhanced security for U.S. military bases and other homeland security that was launched in response to the attacks and continues at a modest level; and
- Operation Inherent Resolve (OIR), authorized by the President on August 7, 2014, beginning with DOD air strikes in Iraq and Syria to "degrade and ultimately defeat" the Islamic State (IS) without deploying U.S. ground troops.

On May 27, 2014, President Obama's announced that the number of U.S. troops in Afghanistan would decrease from 33,000 to 9,800 by January 1, 2015; would halve again by January 1, 2016, to about 4,900; and be limited to an embassy presence of about 1,000 thereafter.[1] Some unspecified number of the 60,000 U.S. troops currently providing in-theater support would remain in the region as an "enduring presence" after the withdrawal of troops from Afghanistan.

THE FY2015 REQUEST AND POTENTIAL WAR COST ISSUES

In June 2014, after the announcement of troop levels for the Afghan withdrawal, the Administration replaced its earlier $79.4 billion placeholder request for DOD (submitted with the original FY2015 budget in March) with an amended war request of $58.6 billion. [2] Including this amended DOD request with State Department/U.S. Agency for International Development (USAID), and Veterans Administration (VA(Medical requests, the total FY2015 war request—including the new November 2014 request for OIR—totals $79.0 billion.

The FY2015 Continuing Resolution (H.J.Res. 124/P.L. 113-164) sets war spending levels for this fiscal year at $95.5 billion, reflecting the FY2014 enacted level. That total is $16.5 billion above the $79.0 billion amended request that includes OIR. The continuing resolution (CR) exceeds the request primarily because DOD's FY2015 request is below the FY2014 enacted level.[3] The CR expires on December 11, 2014, and Congress is expected to pass another CR or an Omnibus Appropriations act to set final FY2015 spending levels.

At that time, Congress may consider the following war budget issues:

- the amount, purposes, and appropriateness of the FY2015 Department of Defense (DOD) war cost request reflecting the troop drawdown to 9,800 troops in December 2014;
- the utility of an Administration proposal for $5 billion for the Counterterrorism Partnerships Fund (CTFP), a broadly-flexible new account intended to respond to "evolving threats" primarily through "Train and Equip" programs;[4]
- whether to rely on OCO-designated funding for all DOD expenses, including paying for an "enduring presence" of some 60,000 U.S. troops in the region, and financing Afghan security forces rather than transferring some of these costs to DOD's base budget; and

- responding to the new November funding request of $5.5 billion for Operation Inherent Resolve, including whether to set restrictions on the use of U.S. ground forces.

These defense budget issues are discussed below after a summary of the status of the FY2015 request and an accounting of cumulative and annual war funding levels for FY2001-FY2015.

Status of FY2015 DOD Request

Under the FY2015 Continuing Resolution or CR (H.J.Res. 124/P.L. 113-164), enacted September 19, 2014, OCO-designated funding would total $95.5 billion. This total includes $85.8 billion for DOD, $21.7 billion above the amended request of $64.1 billion including OIR. After the CR expires on December 11, 2014, Congress is expected to pass either another CR or an Omnibus Appropriations Act that could adjust these levels. Since it is not clear, at this time, whether Congress will address the $5.5 billion amended request for OIR during the lame duck session and whether those funds should appropriately be allocated to Iraq, CRS tables that follow exclude that amount.

FY2015 Defense Authorization Action

The House-passed version of H.R. 4435, the FY2014 National Defense Authorization Act (NDAA), included $79.4 billion for DOD war funding, matching the OCO placeholder request included in the Administration's original FY2015 budget.[7] The House NDAA also adopted an amendment that required that the Administration's war funding request meet OMB's 2010 criteria for DOD war funding that placed certain limitations on what would be considered war-related (see "War Funding and Budget Controls").

Box A. Other CRS Reports and Definitions of War Funding

This CRS report defines war costs as those designated as emergency or OCO appropriations for: Operation Enduring Freedom (OEF) largely for the Afghan war; Operation Iraqi Freedom (OIF) and Operation New Dawn (OND) for Iraq; and, Enhanced Security or Operation Noble Eagle.

For State Department, and USAID, CRS includes all appropriations for activities and programs in Iraq and Afghanistan. CRS includes Budget Authority (BA) for VA Medical costs for OEF/OIF veterans as identified in budget justification materials. Emergency or OCO-designated funds are exempt from budget caps.

Other observers and analysts define war costs more broadly than congressional appropriations and include estimates of the life-time costs of caring for OEF/OIF/OND veterans, imputed interest costs on the deficit, or increases in DOD's base budget deemed to be a consequence of support for the war.[5] Such costs are difficult to compute, subject to extensive caveats, and often based on methodologies that may not be appropriate.[6]

For a discussion of war funding issues for the State Department/USAID FY2015 request, see CRS Report R43569, *State, Foreign Operations, and Related Programs: FY2015 Budget and Appropriations*, by Susan B. Epstein, Alex Tiersky, and Marian L. Lawson. For a description of politico-military developments in Afghanistan and Iraq, see CRS Report RL31339, *Iraq: Post-Saddam Governance and Security*, by Kenneth Katzman, and CRS Report RL30588, *Afghanistan: Post-Taliban Governance, Security, and U.S. Policy*, by Kenneth Katzman. For the Islamic State crisis, see CRS Report IF00050, *The Islamic State: Q&A (In Focus)*, by Carla E. Humud, Christopher M. Blanchard, and Kenneth Katzman and CRS Report R43612, *The "Islamic State" Crisis and U.S. Policy*, by Kenneth Katzman et al., and CRS Report R43727, *Proposed Train and Equip Authorities for Syria: In Brief*, by Christopher M. Blanchard and Amy Belasco.

Table 1. FY2015 National Defense Authorization Act (H.R. 4435/S. 2410)

Subcommittee Markup							Conference Report Approval		
House	Senate	House Report	House Passage	Senate Report	Senate Passage	Conf. Report	House	Senate	Public Law
4/30/2014 and 5/1/2014	na	H.Rept. 113-446 5/8/2014	Passed 325-98 5/22/14	S.Rept. 113-176 6/2/2014			H.R. 3979 12-2-14		

Sources: H.R. 4435 and H.Rept. 113-446 and S. 2410 and S.Rept. 113-176.

Reported on June 2, 2014, the Senate Armed Services Committee version of the FY2015 National Defense Authorization Act (S. 1970) did not address either the placeholder OCO request or the amended request submitted on June 14, 2014. The Senate has not taken up S. 1970 (**Table 1**).

The House passed a conference version of the NDAA, H.R. 3979, on December 4, 2014, and the Senate is expected to consider it prior to the adjournment of the 113th Congress. With the exception of the request for Counterterrorism Partnership Response Fund (CTPF), H.R. 3779 made minor adjustments to DOD's entire OCO-designated request. The conference bill reduces the $4.0 billion DOD request to $1.3 billion. The final NDAA will set a cap on funding levels.

Although H.R. 3979 approves the $1.618 billion requested for a new Iraq Train and Equip account, it makes several revisions, including sunsetting the authority on December 31, 2016, rather than September 30, 2017.

The bill endorses the Administration cost-sharing provision in which U.S. obligations are capped at 60% until Iraqi, Kurdish, and tribal security forces contribute 40% of the $1.6 billion total, in cash or in kind.[8]

The conference draft also sets a 25% cap on obligations and expenditures that would go into effect 15 days after the Secretary of Defense and the Secretary of State submit a specific plan identifying, to the appropriate congressional committee and the House and Senate leadership, the forces to receive assistance and the retraining and rebuilding for those forces. The plan is to include goals, concept of operations, timelines, types of training and other assistances, roles of other partners, number and roles of U.S. military personnel, and additional military support and sustainment, and other relevant details. Ninety days later, and every 30 days thereafter, the Secretary of Defense is to submit quarterly reports of any changes.[9]

Instead of the blank waiver of other laws requested, H.R. 3979 permits more limited waiver authority for the Secretary of Defense of acquisition and arms sales provisions. It also includes a more general waiver for the President if it is determined to be vital to U.S. national security, and it can be implemented only 15 days after notification to the appropriate defense committees.[10]

H.R. 3979 also continues the Continuing Resolution provision that funds training of vetted Syrian opposition forces by reprogramming from other funds. The bill also rejected the broad authorities requested, and included additional reporting requirements for both the Iraq and the Syria Train and Equip programs.[11]

FY2015 Defense Appropriations Action

The House passed H.R. 4870, the FY2015 DOD Appropriations Act on June 20, 2014, providing OCO-designated funding of $79.4 billion, matching the Administration's placeholder request. Funding levels were set at the title level (Military Personnel, Operation and Maintenance) rather than by account, as is customary.

The Senate Appropriations Committee version of H.R. 4870 provided $58.3 billion for DOD, close to the amended request of $58.6 billion; the Senate version added about $1 billion to both Operation and Maintenance and procurement accounts that was offset by halving the $4.0 billion requested for the new flexible Counterterrorism Response Program (CTRP) that would give the Administration broad discretion to provide funds to countries conducting counter-terror efforts (see **Table 2** and **Figure 9**).

The section below summarizes cumulative war funding by operation and agency. It also analyzes the major factors affecting annual funding levels. The tables below do not reflect the $5.5 billion budget amendment to combat the Islamic State, considered to be a new operation by the Department of Defense. That request is discussed separately in the section titled "The New Request to Counter the Islamic State."

Table 2. FY2015 DOD Appropriations Bill (H.R. 4870)

Subcommittee Markup		House Report	House Passage	Senate Report	Senate Passage	Conf. Report	Conference Report Approval		
House	Senate						House	Senate	Public Law
5/30/2014/	7/15/2014	H.Rept. 113-473 6/13/2014	Passed 340-73 6/20/14	S.Rept. 113-211 7/17/2014					

Sources: H.R. 4870 as passed by the House and reported by the Senate Appropriations Committee; H.Rept. 113-473 and S.Rept. 113-211.

CUMULATIVE WAR FUNDING AND THE FY2015 REQUEST

Based on funding enacted from the 9/11 attacks through FY2014, CRS estimates a total of $1.6 trillion has been provided to the Department of Defense, the State Department and the Department of Veterans Administration for war operations, diplomatic operations and foreign aid, and medical care for Iraq and Afghan war veterans over the past 13 years of war.

By Operation

Allocated by operation, this $1.6 trillion total is made up of:

- $686 billion for Afghanistan and other counter-terror operations (OEF);
- $815 billion for Iraq (OIF);
- $27 billion for enhanced security (Operation Noble Eagle); and
- $81 billion in other spending designated as war funding but tangentiallyrelated to the Afghan and Iraq war (**Table 3**).[12]

Table 3. Cumulative War Funding by Operation, FY2001-FY2015 Request In Billions of Dollars of Budget Authority (BA) and Percent of Total

Fiscal Year/ Operation	Cumulative Total					
	In Billions of $			As Percent of Total		
	FY01-14 Enacted	FY2015 Request[a]	FY2001-15 Request[a]	FY01-14 Enacted	FY2015 Request[a]	FY01-15 Request[a]
Afghanistan/ OEF[b]	$685.6	$58.1	$743.7	43%	79%	44%
Iraq/OIF/ OND[c]	$814.6	$5.0	$819.6	51%	7%	49%
Enhanced Security[d]	$27.4	$0.1	$27.5	2%	0%	2%
Other[e]	$81.3	$10.4	$91.7	5%	14%	5%
Total	**$1,608.9**	**$73.5**	**$1,682.4**	**100%**	**100%**	**100%**

Sources: Relevant public laws, House Appropriation Committee tables, conference reports for relevant appropriations acts for State/USAID and VA Medical, For DOD, CRS calculates splits by operation using DOD's Cumulative CW-01-Z data base which reports obligations by operation, fiscal year, account, and type of expense. In addition to obligations incurred, in more recent years, CRS estimates unobligated balances based on DOD data on shares by appropriation account; for the FY2015 request, CRS uses figures shown in Department of Defense, *Fiscal Year 2015 Budget Amendment, Overview, Overseas Contingency Operations, June 2014;* http://comptroller.defense.gov/Portals/45/Documents/defbudget/

fy2015/amendment/ FY2015_Budget_Request_Overview_Book_Amended.pdf. State Department/USAID figures reflect enacted levels and FY2015 request based on appropriation reports, budget justification materials on allocations between operations, a USAID data base (the "spigot" table), and State Department materials. VA figures are from annual budget justification materials for Medical Funding; allocated between operations by CRS based on a cumulative rolling average reflecting in-country troop levels. Excludes OIR. Total percentages may not equal 100 due to rounding.

Of the total amount appropriated,:

- 43% for the Afghan war;
- 51% for the Iraq war;
- 2% for enhanced security; and
- 5% for "Other war spending," by DOD and the State Department designated for war but not part of war operations or direct support (see **Table 3** and "War Funding and Budget Controls").

As would be expected, the majority of the FY2015 request is for the war in Afghanistan with

- $58.1 billion for Afghanistan/OEF;
- $5.0 billion for Iraq/OIF/OND;
- $100 million for enhanced security; and
- $10.4 billion for other war-designated costs that are not directly part of war operations or aid to Afghanistan or Iraq.

If Congress approves the FY2015 war funding request for $73.5 billion for DOD, State/USAID, and VA Medical (excluding the new OIR request), cumulative funding over the past 15 years would rise to $1.69 trillion, including $744 billion for Afghanistan/OEF, $820 billion for Iraq/OIF/OND, $28 billion for Enhanced Security, and $92 billion in "Other" funding (**Table 3**).

"Other" War Funding

In this report, CRS war funding totals include all funding designated by statute as for emergencies or for Overseas Contingency Operations or for Afghanistan and Iraq.[13] Of the $1.6 trillion total for FY2001-FY2015 request (excluding OIR), "other" war funding designated as emergency or OCO but not directly related to Afghan or Iraq war operations, diplomatic support, or foreign aid to Afghanistan or Iraq countries totals $91 billion or about 5.4% of the total (see **Table 3** and "Changes in DOD Definitions of War Funding").[14]

By Agency

Splitting the cumulative total of $1.6 trillion (excluding OIR) appropriated by agency:

- $1.5 trillion was appropriated to DOD;
- $92.7 billion to State/USAID, and
- $17.6 billion to the Veterans Administration (VA) for medical treatment[15]

In terms of shares for the three agencies:

- 92% was appropriated to the Department of Defense for military operations and support and training Afghan and Iraq forces;
- 6% for the State/USAID reconstruction and foreign aid programs; and
- 1% for VA Medical funding for OEF/OIF/OND veterans (**Table 4**).

By agency, the FY2015 war request includes:

- $58.6 billion for the Department of Defense;
- $9.4 billion for State Department/U.S.AID; and
- $5.2 billion for VA Medical.

By shares, in the FY2015 request:

- 80% is for DOD;
- 13% for State/USAID, higher than the cumulative share; and
- 7% for VA Medical, also above the cumulative share (**Table 4**).

Table 4. Cumulative War Funding by Agency, FY2001-FY2015 Request In Billions of Dollars of Budget Authority (BA) and Percent of Total

Fiscal year/ Agency	Cumulative Total: In Billions of $			Cumulative Total: As Percent of Total		
	FY2001-FY2014 Enacted	FY2015 Request[a]	FY2001-FY2015 Request[a]	FY2001-FY2014 Enacted	FY2015 Request[a]	FY2001-FY2015 Request[a]
DOD	$1,498.7	$58.6	$1,557.6	92%	80%	93%
State/USAID	$92.7	$9.4	$102.1	6%	13%	6%
VA Medical	$17.6	$5.2	$22.8	1%	7%	1%
Total	**$1,608.9**	**$73.5**	**$1,682.4**	**100.0%**	**100%**	**100%**

Sources: Relevant public laws, House Appropriation Committee tables, conference reports for relevant appropriations acts for State/USAID and VA Medical, For DOD, CRS relies on DOD's Cumulative CW-01-Z data base, which reports obligations by operation, fiscal year, account, and type of expense. In addition to obligations incurred, in more recent years, CRS estimates unobligated balances based on DOD data on shares by appropriation account; for the FY2015 request, CRS uses figures shown in Department of Defense, *Fiscal Year 2015 Budget Amendment, Overview, Overseas Contingency Operations, June 2014;* http://comptroller.defense.gov/Portals/45/Documents/defbudget/fy2015/amendment/FY2015_Budget_Request_Overview_Book_Amended.pdf. State Department/ USAID figures reflect enacted levels and FY2015 request based on appropriation reports, budget justification materials on allocations between operations, and a USAID data base (the "spigot" table). VA figures are from annual budget justification materials for VA Medical programs.

Notes: Totals may not add due to rounding. Excludes OIR.

DOD funds are used to conduct and support military operations and reset damaged or destroyed equipment, to train the Afghan and Iraq security forces, and to provide other assistance for reconstruction, coalition support, and counter-drug operations. State Department funding is for the conduct of diplomatic operations and foreign assistance programs ranging from the Economic Support Fund to counter-drug programs. VA medical funding provides for medical care of OEF/OIF/OND veterans; this does not include the cost of VA disability payments because VA does not provide those figures.[16]

U.S. Boots on the Ground, FY2001-FY2015

Although there are other significant variables, the main factor in determining costs is the number of U.S. troops deployed to Afghanistan and Iraq at different points in time. Between 2001 and 2014, troop levels in Iraq and in Afghanistan changed dramatically. Because policy announcements typically focus on "Boots on the Ground" in-country, **Figure 1** shows those figures and excludes military personnel providing support in the region or conducting other counter-terrorism operations (see **Figure 2**).

For FY2002-FY2007, overall troop levels reflect the combined effect of the gradual buildup in U.S. troop levels in Afghanistan after the 9/11 attacks and the Iraq invasion in 2003, followed by the Iraq surge ordered by then-President George W. Bush from 2007-2008. The next phase includes the phased withdrawal for Iraq by December 2012 and the gradual buildup resulting from the troop surge in Afghanistan initiated by then-President Bush in 2008 and continued by President Obama in 2009. That surge peaked in May 2011 and was followed by a phased withdrawal that is to culminate in January 2017 with a limited embassy presence (**Figure 1**).

Changing Troop Levels in Iraq, 2003-2014

Six months after the invasion of Iraq in March 2003, U.S. troop levels reached 149,000 troops in- country. By December 2003, troop levels fell to 124,000 and remained at about that level for the next three years. In January 2007, then-President Bush initiated the Iraq surge in response to growing levels of violence and a request for assistance in fighting insurgents, referred to as the "Sunni Awakening." The "Iraq surge" peaked at 165,000 troops in November 2007. As levels of violence fell by July 2008, then-President Bush began to reverse the surge and troop levels declined to 147,000 (**Figure 1**).

After President Obama took office in January 2009, the Administration conducted a strategy review of both the Afghan and Iraq wars. In that review, the President decided to shift U.S. forces in Iraq from a combat to an advisory and assistance role, and reduce troop levels from 141,000 in March 2009 to about 50,000 by September 2010. The bilateral security agreement at that time required that all U.S. troops be withdrawn by December 31, 2011. Although the United States hoped to revise that agreement and retain some troops beyond 2011, the Iraqi government refused to sign a new agreement that would shield U.S. troops from local law, so all U.S. troops were withdrawn by December 31, 2011. There are currently 100 to 200 U.S. military personnel in Iraq to manage arms sales.[17]

In thousands of U.S. troops

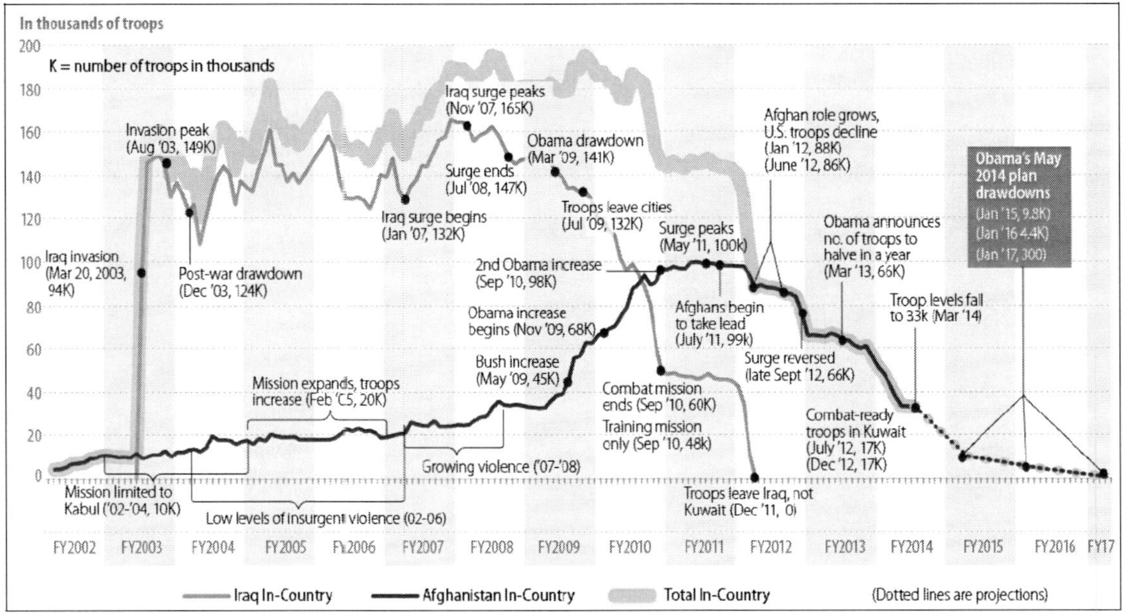

Sources: DOD, Monthly Boots-on-the Ground reports provided to CRS and congressional defense committees, 2001-June 2014. For month-by-month troop levels, both in-country and in-theater, see Table A-1.

Notes: Reflects U.S. troops in-country; excludes troops providing in-theater support or conducting counter-terror operations outside the region.

Figure 1. Boots on the Ground In-Country, FY2001-FY2017.

Changing Troop Levels in Afghanistan, 2001-2017

Compared to Iraq, troop strength in Afghanistan grew more slowly but is falling as rapidly. After the initial defeat of the Taliban in December 2001, the number of U.S. troops gradually doubled from 10,000 in 2002 to 20,000 in 2005 as the mission expanded, although violence remained at a fairly low level. In response to concerns about the deteriorating security situation raised by U.S. commanding officers, then-President Bush agreed to gradually double U.S. troop levels to about 40,000 between 2007 and 2008. Before leaving office in 2009, then-President Bush agreed to increase U.S. troops in Afghanistan to 45,000, initiating what became known as the Afghanistan surge.[18]

After its strategy review, the new administration decided to continue the surge and add another 20,000 troops by November 2009. After a second review in December 2009 prompted by pressure from military commanders for additional troops to combat worsening security, President Obama approved an additional increase of 30,000 troops, bringing the total number of U.S. total to 98,000 by September 2010.[19] At that time, President Obama committed to evaluate current U.S. strategy in Afghanistan in December 2010 to "allow us to begin the transfer of our forces out of Afghanistan in July of 2011."[20] The total peaked at 100,000 in May 2011 (**Figure 1**).

On July 22, 2011, President Obama announced the surge would be reversed and the U.S. role would transition from a combat role to a train and assist role in Afghanistan, stating that by "2014, this process of transition will be complete, and the Afghan people will be responsible for their own security." As Afghan troops gradually took the lead, U.S. troop levels declined fairly rapidly from the May 2011 peak of 100,000 to about 65,000 in September 2012. In February 2013, President Obama announced that the number of U.S. troops in Afghanistan would halve from 65,000 to 33,000 within a year. The President also announced that the "drawdown will continue and by the end of next year, our war in Afghanistan will be over."[21]

After over a year of speculation about future U.S. troop levels in Afghanistan, President Obama announced on May 27, 2014, that once the U.S. combat role ended by December 31, 2014, some 9,800 troops would remain for another year to train Afghan security forces and conduct counter-terror operations. That number would halve to about 4,900 by January 2016, and fall to "an embassy presence" by January 2017.[22]

This plan was contingent on the Afghan government signing a new bilateral security agreement (BSA) with Afghanistan which would shield U.S. troops from Afghan law, a U.S. precondition, and possibly specify the size and role of the residual force and U.S. funding support for Afghan Security Forces, subject to congressional appropriations. [23] Although then-President Karzai was unwilling to sign the agreement, his successor, President Ashraf Ghani signed the agreement on September 30, 2014, the day after taking office.[24] The new BSA does not specify U.S. troop levels or require that the United States remain in Afghanistan after 2014 or provide for permanent U.S. bases in Afghanistan.[25]

NATO and Afghan Troops

In addition to U.S. troops, some 28 NATO and other allies have also deployed troops to Afghanistan as part of the International Security Assistance Force (ISAF). Between 2001 and 2008, these allies contributed roughly the same number of troops as the United States. During the Afghan surge, that ratio dropped to 50% and has remained at roughly that level since then.[26]

Location of U.S. Military Personnel Serving in OEF and OIF/OND

Figure 2 shows the number and location of U.S. military personnel serving in either OEF or OIF/OND as of March 2014 based on DOD documents. As points of comparison, it also shows the number of U.S. military personnel deployed in the region before 9/11, at the peak of the Iraq surge in 2008 and the Afghan surge in 2011. These figures differ from the more-commonly cited "boots on the ground" numbers that include only U.S. military personnel in-country, in Afghanistan, and in Iraq. The additional personnel shown include those military personnel providing "in-theater support," those engaged in other counter-terrorism operations, and those deployed on ships afloat.

Before the 9/11 attacks, the number of U.S. military personnel in the Area of Operations (AOR) for OEF, OIF, and OND totaled some 30,000 including about 15,000 on ships afloat in the region. During the Iraq surge of April 2008, U.S. personnel reached a peak of just over 300,000, a 10-fold increase. That total included some 53,000 for OEF and about 224,000 for OIF as well as 17,000 on ships afloat (**Figure 2**).

In May 2011, during the Afghan surge, the number of U.S. military personnel peaked at 278,000, somewhat below the Iraq surge. That total included 156,000 for OEF, another 86,000 for OIF, and 30,000 afloat. By the end of December 2011, all U.S. troops were withdrawn from Iraq and the Iraq mission (OND) ended. After December 2011, troops providing in-theater support for Iraq were transferred to OEF because of the end of the Iraq mission.[27]

In 2000, 2008, 2011, and 2014

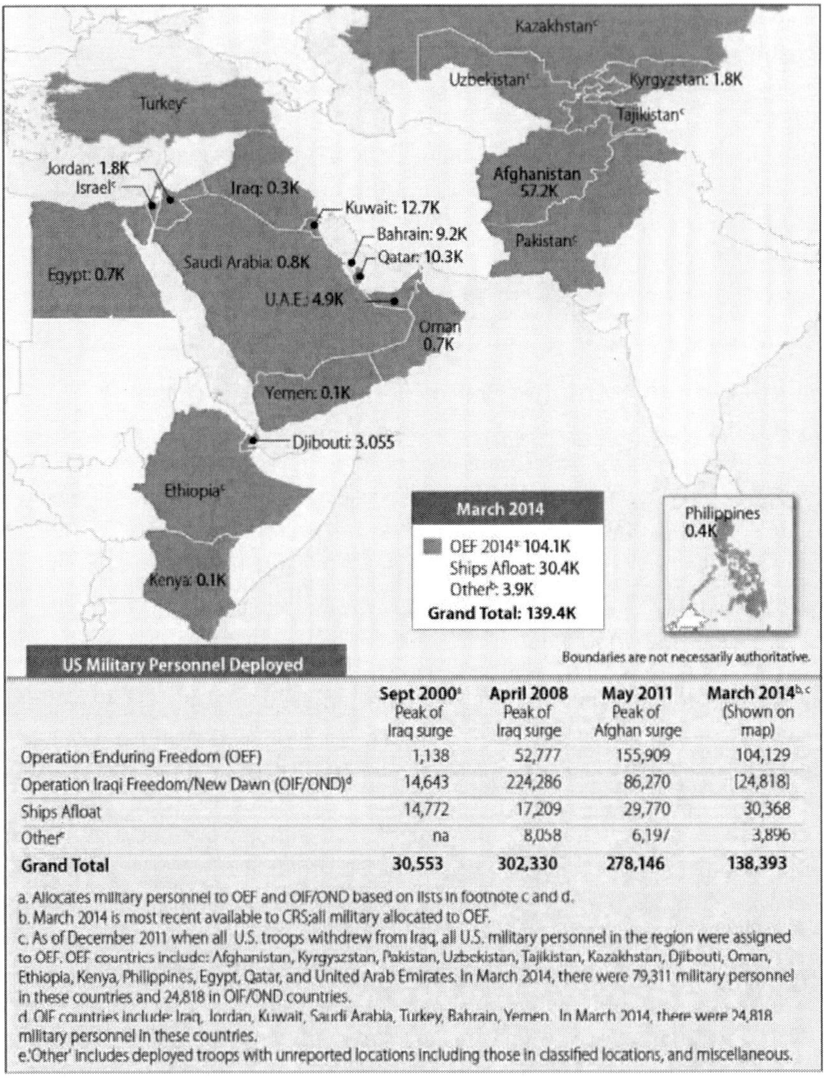

US Military Personnel Deployed

	Sept 2000[a] Peak of Iraq surge	April 2008 Peak of Iraq surge	May 2011 Peak of Afghan surge	March 2014[b,c] (Shown on map)
Operation Enduring Freedom (OEF)	1,138	52,777	155,909	104,129
Operation Iraqi Freedom/New Dawn (OIF/OND)[d]	14,643	224,286	86,270	[24,818]
Ships Afloat	14,772	17,209	29,770	30,368
Other[e]	na	8,058	6,197	3,896
Grand Total	**30,553**	**302,330**	**278,146**	**138,393**

a. Allocates military personnel to OEF and OIF/OND based on lists in footnote c and d.
b. March 2014 is most recent available to CRS;all military allocated to OEF.
c. As of December 2011 when all U.S. troops withdrew from Iraq, all U.S. military personnel in the region were assigned to OEF. OEF countries include: Afghanistan, Kyrgyszstan, Pakistan, Uzbekistan, Tajikistan, Kazakhstan, Djibouti, Oman, Ethiopia, Kenya, Philippines, Egypt, Qatar, and United Arab Emirates. In March 2014, there were 79,311 military personnel in these countries and 24,818 in OIF/OND countries.
d. OIF countries include: Iraq, Jordan, Kuwait, Saudi Arabia, Turkey, Bahrain, Yemen. In March 2014, there were 24,818 military personnel in these countries.
e.'Other' includes deployed troops with unreported locations including those in classified locations, and miscellaneous.

Sources: For 2001, Department of Defense, Active Duty Military Personnel Strengths by Regional Area and By Country (309A), September 200 I; https://www.dmdc.

osd.mil/appj/dwp/reports.do?c.ategory=reports&subCat=milActDutReg; Defense Manpower Data Center, DRS 11280–Number of Members Deployed By Country, By Component and Month/Years, Contingency Tracking System file as of March 31, 2014.

Figure 2. OEF and OIF Deployed U.S. Troops.

By March 2014, the total U.S. military personnel assigned to OEF had dropped to 138,000, reflecting the drawdown in Afghanistan (**Figure 2**).

Trends in War Funding by Operation

From the 9/11 attacks until FY2008, total war costs for all three operations—Iraq, Afghanistan, and other GWOT and enhanced security—rose steeply from $36 billion in FY2001/FY2002 to a peak of $195 billion in FY2008, primarily because of Iraq war costs. In FY2009, overall war funding fell to $157 billion, reflecting the decline in troop levels after the Iraq surge, and the beginning of troop withdrawals.

The decline of total war costs since FY008 due to the Iraq withdrawal was partly offset by the rise in Afghan war costs because of the FY2009-FY2011 troop surge in Afghanistan. In FY2001/FY2002, the cost of enhanced security (Operation Noble Eagle) covered the initial responses to the 9/11 attacks, repair of the Pentagon, and combat air patrols in the United States. These costs declined, falling to less than $200 million by FY2008 (**Figure 3**).

Iraq War Funding

As troop levels in Iraq rose to 149,000 after the invasion in the spring of 2003, war funding for the year reached $51 billion, rising further to $77 billion in FY2004 and to $79 billion in FY2005 as the United States established bases in Iraq to support somewhat lower troop levels. With the initiation of the surge in 2007, costs increased to $131 billion, then peaked at $144 billion in FY2008.

With the reversal of the Iraq surge, Iraq costs declined to $93 billion in FY2009, $65 billion in FY2010. As the U.S. combat mission was replaced with an "advise and assist" role, costs continued to fall to $47 billion in FY2011, and $20 billion in FY2012 when all U.S. troops were withdrawn (**Figure 1** and **Figure 3**).

Afghan War Funding

After dropping from $23 billion in FY2002 to $17 billion in FY2003 and $15 billion in FY2004, Afghan war costs rose to $19 billion in FY2005 and $31 billion in FY2006 with troop levels around 20,000. By FY2008, Afghan costs increased to $39 billion as both troop levels and the conflict's intensity grew. With the initiation of the Afghan troop surge, costs grew to $56 billion in FY2009, and $94 billion in FY2010, peaking at $107 billion in FY2011 (**Figure 3**).

In Billions of Dollars of Budget Authority

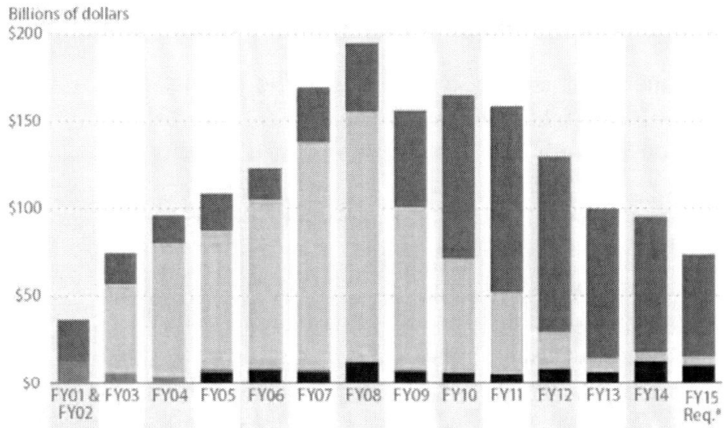

Operation	FY01 & FY02	FY03	FY04	FY05	FY06	FY07	FY08	FY09	FY10	FY11	FY12	FY13	FY14	FY15 Req.*	Cumulative Enacted*
Afghanistan/ OEF[b]	$23	$17	$15	$21	$19	$31	$39	$56	$94	$107	$101	$86	$77	$58	**$686**
Iraq/ OIF/OND[c]	$0	$51	$77	$79	$96	$131	$144	$93	$65	$47	$20	$8	$5	$5	**$815**
Enhanced Security[d]	$13	$6	$4	$2	$1	$1	$**	$**	$**	$**	$**	$**	$**	$**	**$27**
Other[e]	$0	$0	$0	$7	$8	$7	$12	$7	$6	$5	$9	$7	$13	$10	**$81**
Total	$36	$74	$96	$108	$124	$170	$195	$157	$165	$159	$130	$100	$95	$74	**$1,609**

* Cumulative enacted (FY01-FY14). ** Amounts less than $200 million.

Sources: Relevant public laws, House Appropriation Committee tables on relevant appropriations acts, DOD budget justification material, DOD, Cumulative CW-01-Z, Cumulative (war obligations data base), March and June 2014. DOD figures are split by operation based on obligations incurred for each operation for funds of each fiscal year; State Department/USAID figures reflect enacted levels, and budget justification material on allocations between operations; VA from annual budget justification materials for Medical Funding; allocated between operations by CRS based on a cumulative rolling average of in-country troop levels.

Notes:

a. FY2015 reflects June 2014 amended request rather than initial placeholder request of $79.4 billion for DOD; reflects resources not scoring level. Excludes $5.5 billion requested for OIR in FY2015.

b. DOD refers to the Afghan war as Operation Enduring Freedom (OEF), primarily military and other operations in Afghanistan as well as in-theater support in neighboring countries and other counter-terror operations (e.g., Philippines, Djibouti).

c. DOD refers to the Iraq war as Operation Iraqi Freedom (OIF) until September 1, 2010, when U.S. forces transitioned from combat operations to advising, assisting, and training Iraqi forces and the mission was re- named Operation New Dawn (OND). OND ended on December 31, 2011 when all U.S. forces left the country of Iraq; military personnel continuing to provide in-theater support were assigned to OEF. Excludes new OIR request.

d. Enhanced security covers cost of 9/11 attacks to the Department of Defense (DOD) and in New York City; referred to as Noble Eagle by DOD.

e. "Other" includes funding in DOD designated as for war emergency or for Overseas Contingency Operations (OCO) that is not tracked by DOD as a war cost, such as congressional adds for childcare centers, barracks improvements, additional C-130 and C-17 aircraft not requested as well as unanticipated increases in basic housing allowances, fuel costs, modularity or restructuring of Army brigades, and in recent years, transfers by Congress of base budget operation and maintenance expenses to Title IX war funding.

Figure 3. Estimated War Funding by Operation, FY2001-FY2015 Request.

As U.S. troop levels declined and Afghan forces have taken the lead in operations, U.S. costs dropped to $86 billion in FY2013 and $77 billion in FY2014. The current FY2015 request is $58 billion for Afghanistan expenses for DOD, State/USAID, and VA Medical. In addition to higher troop strength, cost increases reflect substantial amounts to train Afghan security forces and higher investment levels in response to policy changes.

Enhanced Security

Funding for Enhanced Security (Operation Noble Eagle) peaked at $13 billion in the first year after the 9/11 attacks, primarily for one-time costs like Pentagon reconstruction ($1.3 billion), security upgrades, combat air patrol (about $1.3 billion for around-the-clock coverage), and activating reservists to guard bases.[28] These costs fell to $4 billion in 2003, and then to $2 billion in FY2004.

Beginning in FY2005, DOD funded this operation in its baseline budget rather than as emergency or Overseas Contingency Operation (OCO) funding. Costs fell to under $1 billion in FY2006, $500 million in FY2007, and about $100 million per year in FY2008 and after (**Figure 3**).

Trends in War Funding by Agency

The Department of Defense accounts for $1.5 trillion or 92% of the $1.6 trillion total enacted war funding. Diplomatic operations and foreign aid programs of the State Department account for another $93 billion, or 6% of the total. Another $18 billion, or just over 1% of war funding, funds medical care in the Department of Veterans Affairs (VA) for OEF and OIF veterans. The VA does not provide figures showing the cost of its benefits for veterans of the two wars (**Figure 4**).

Department of Defense

DOD's war funding for the Afghan and Iraq wars primarily pays for deploying and supporting U.S. troops (e.g., special pays for deployed personnel), conducting and supporting military operations, repairing war-worn equipment, and transporting troops and equipment to and from the war zone (O&M activities); buying and upgrading weapon systems (Procurement); conducting Research, Development, and Testing and Evaluation (RDT&E); Military Construction on site; and conducting intelligence activities. In addition, DOD war funding finances training for the Afghan and Iraqi security forces and other reconstruction activities.

DOD funding grew more rapidly than might have been expected based on changes in troop levels alone. Instead, much of the increase reflects other factors discussed below—higher than anticipated support costs, an expanded definition of war-related procurement, and the growth of programs to meet specific needs, such as training Afghan and Iraqi security forces.

State Department Diplomatic Operations and U.S. Foreign Aid (USAID)

The $93 billion in war appropriations enacted thus far for the State Department/USAID funds diplomatic operations: e.g., paying staff, providing security, building and maintaining embassies, and funding a variety of foreign aid programs in Afghanistan and Iraq ranging from the Economic Support Fund to counter-drug activities.[29] This figure reflects all funds for Afghanistan and Iraq provided in the regular base budget or as emergency or OCO-designated appropriations.

In Billions of Dollars of Budget Authority

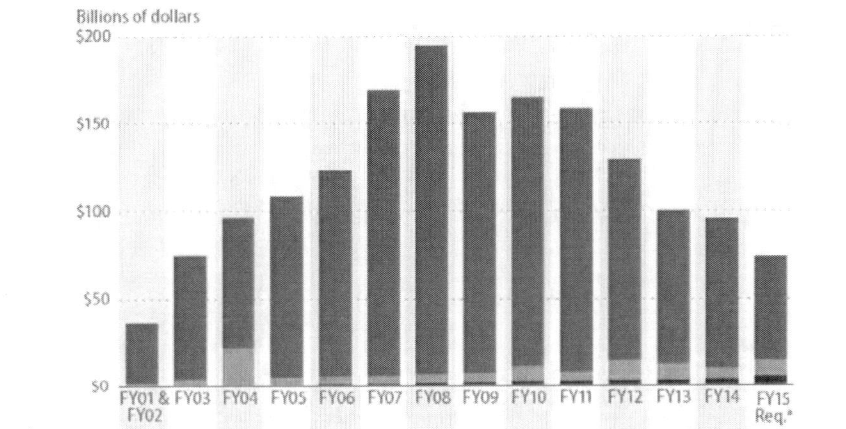

Agency	FY01 & FY02	FY03	FY04	FY05	FY06	FY07	FY08	FY09	FY10	FY11	FY12	FY13	FY14	FY15 Req.*	Cumulative Enacted*
DOD	$35	$71	$74	$104	$118	$164	$189	$150	$155	$151	$115	$87	$85	$59	**$1,499**
State/USAID	$1	$4	$22	$5	$5	$5	$5	$5	$9	$5	$11	$9	$6	$9	**$93**
VA Medical	$0	$0	$0	$0	**	$1	$1	$1	$2	$2	$3	$3	$4	$5	**$18**
Total	$36	$74	$96	$108	$124	$170	$195	$157	$165	$159	$130	$100	$95	$74	**$1,609**

* Cumulative enacted (FY01-FY14). ** Amounts less than $500 million.

Source: Relevant public laws, House Appropriation Committee tables on relevant appropriations acts, DOD budget justification material, DOD, Cumulative CW-01-Z, Cumulative (war obligations data base), March and June 2014. DOD figures are split by operation based on obligations incurred for each operation for funds of each fiscal year; State Department/USAID figures reflect enacted levels, and budget justification material on allocations between operations; VA budget justification materials for each year.

Notes: FY2015 reflects June 2014 amended request rather than initial placeholder request of $79.4 billion for DOD. Excludes $5.5 billion requested for OIR in FY2015.

Figure 4. Estimated War Funding by Agency, FY2001-FY2015 Request.

Starting in FY2012, the State Department, like DOD, began to designate certain monies in its regular request as OCO, to fund

> the extraordinary, but temporary, costs of the Department of State and the U.S. Agency for International Development (USAID) operations in the Frontline States of Iraq, Afghanistan, and Pakistan... [identifying] the exceptional costs of operating in these countries that are focal points of U.S national security policy [as opposed to] the permanent base requirements in the Frontline States, which will endure after OCO funding is phased out.[30]

Except for a one-time appropriation of $20 billion for Iraq reconstruction in FY2004, war-related annual foreign aid and diplomatic operations funding hovered between $4 billion and $5 billion each year until FY2011 with one exception in FY2010. When the State Department began to designate spending as OCO, funding levels rose to $11 billion in FY2012 and $9 billion in FY2013, partly due the budgetary advantage of the designation which exempts this funding from budget limits. State/USAID funding fell to $6 billion in FY2014 (**Figure 4**).[31]

In its FY2015 request of $14 billion, the State Department gives another rationale for OCO- designated funding—"an important tool that allows the Department to deal with extraordinary activities that are critical to our immediate national security objectives without unnecessarily undermining funding for our longer-term efforts to sustain global order and tackle transnational challenges."[32]

VA Medical War-Related Funding

The VA identifies the dollar value of all medical services provided to OEF/OIF veterans who qualify for care based on statutory criteria. Costs for VA medical services have increased not only as the number of those eligible grows but also as the criteria for eligibility has expanded since the 9/11 attacks.

In general, veterans who served in combat theater of operations are entitled to five years of VA health care services following their separation from active duty, regardless of whether they are eligible for VA services on other grounds, such as service-related medical condition. For combat veterans who were discharged or released from active service on or after January 28, 2003, they may enroll in the VA health care system within five years from the date of their most recent discharge. [33] Most of VA's medical expenses for OEF/OIF veterans have been funded with regular appropriations. The VA also provides disability benefits to OEF and OIF veterans but has not published the amounts attributable to these veterans.

See **Table 5** for a more detailed breakdown of the cost of the Afghan and Iraq wars.

WAR FUNDING AND BUDGET CONTROLS

Since the 9/11 attacks, some observers have criticized war funding as "off-budget" or a "slush fund" appropriated largely in emergency supplemental acts or for "Overseas Contingency Operations" (OCO) where normal budget limits in annual budget resolutions or the Budget Control Act (BCA) do not apply.[34] In recent testimony on September 18, 2014, for example, former Secretary of Defense Chuck Hagel acknowledged these ambiguities, saying "there're a lot of different opinions about whether there should be an overseas contingency account or not and whether it's a slush fund or not."[35]

Some observers have argued that the tendency to designate funding for activities only tangentially related to OCO or war has intensified with the threat of sequestration in the BCA. Under that act, if final appropriations breach separate, annual "defense" and non-defense budget caps, OMB must administer a largely across-the-board sequestration reducing each account, and sometimes individual programs, by the same percentage to ensure that caps are met.[36] (Should a sequestration be required, however, all budgetary resources, including war funding, would be affected by across-the-board cuts.)

Others have suggested that the "OCO" designation has provided a "safety valve" to preserve base budget programs and help agencies meet BCA caps by designating funding for base budget programs as OCO.[37] For example, Congress transferred $9.2 billion in Operation and Maintenance (O&M) funds from DOD's base budget request to the OCO-designated Title I funds in the FY2014 Consolidated Appropriations Act (P.L. 113-76).[38]

Under the BCA caps, DOD spending has been constrained to $496 billion in FY2013, FY2014, and FY2015, with a $3 billion increase to $499 billion in FY2016.[39] DOD contends that the BCA "sequester" caps (the limits that must be reached to avoid a sequester) would require DOD to make significant cuts from current plans that would affect both readiness and modernization.[40] DOD's current Future Years Defense plan exceeds the BCA limits by $176 billion or 3.3% over the BCA caps between FY2012 and FY2021.[41]

Table 5. Estimated War Funding by Operation, Agency, and Fiscal Year, FY2001-FY2015 Request

In Billions of Dollars of Budget Authority															
Operation/ Agency	**01 &02**	**03**	**04**	**05**	**06**	**07**	**08**	**09**	**10**	**11**	**12**	**13**	**14**	**15 Req.[a]**	**FY 01-14**	**FY 01-15**
Afghan War or Operation Enduring Freedom (OEF)																
DOD	22.0	16.7	13.2	17.9	17.5	29.2	36.1	52.6	88.2	103.1	96.3	80.6	74.0	53.3	**647.3**	**700.7**
State/ USAID	0.8	0.7	2.2	2.8	1.1	1.9	2.7	3.1	5.6	3.3	3.5	3.9	2.0	2.6	**33.6**	**36.2**
VA Medical	0.0	0.0	0.0	0.0	0.1	0.1	0.1	0.2	0.3	0.5	0.8	1.1	1.4	2.2	**4.7**	**6.9**
Total	22.8	17.4	15.4	20.7	18.7	31.1	39.0	56.0	94.1	106.8	100.6	85.6	77.4	58.1	**685.6**	**743.7**
Iraq War or Operation Iraqi Freedom (OIF) and Operation New Dawn (OND)																
DOD	0.0	48.0	57.1	77.1	91.9	127.1	140.3	89.6	59.9	42.7	13.5	4.9	1.1	0.5	**753.1**	**753.5**
State/ USAID	0.0	3.0	19.5	2.0	3.7	3.2	2.7	2.2	3.3	2.1	4.7	0.7	1.4	1.5	**48.6**	**50.2**
VA Medical	0.0	0.0	0.0	0.0	0.4	0.6	0.9	1.3	1.6	1.8	2.1	2.1	2.3	3.0	**12.9**	**15.9**
Total	0.0	51.0	76.7	79.1	96.0	130.8	143.9	93.1	64.8	46.5	20.3	7.7	4.8	5.0	**814.6**	**819.6**
Enhanced Security or Operation Noble Eagle (ONE)																
DOD	13.0	6.0	4.0	2.0	1.0	0.5	0.2	0.2	0.1	0.1	0.2	0.1	0.1	0.1	**27.4**	**27.5**
State/ USAID	13.0	6.0	4.0	2.0	1.0	0.5	0.2	0.2	0.1	0.1	0.2	0.1	0.1	0.1	**27.4**	**27.5**
War-Designated Funding Not War-Related																
DOD	0.0	0.0	0.0	6.6	8.0	7.3	12.1	7.5	6.4	5.4	5.4	1.9	10.2	5.1	**70.9**	**75.9**
State/ USAID	0.0	0.0	0.0	0.0	0.0	0.0	0.0	0.0	0.0	0.0	3.2	4.6	2.6	5.3	**10.4**	**15.7**
Total	0.0	0.0	0.0	6.6	8.0	7.3	12.1	7.5	6.4	5.4	8.6	6.6	12.8	10.4	**81.3**	**91.7**

Operation/ Agency	01 &02	03	04	05	06	07	08	09	10	11	12	13	14	15 Req.[a]	FY 01-14	FY 01-15
All War-Designated Funding																
DOD	35.0	70.7	74.3	103.6	118.4	164.0	188.7	149.8	154.6	151.2	115.3	87.5	85.4	58.9	**1,498.7**	**1,557.6**
State/ USAID	0.8	3.8	21.7	4.8	4.9	5.0	5.4	5.4	8.9	5.4	11.5	9.2	6.0	9.4	**92.7**	**107.1**
VA Medical	0.0	0.0	0.0	0.0	0.4	0.7	1.0	1.5	1.9	2.3	2.9	3.2	3.7	5.2	**17.6**	**22.8**
Total	35.8	74.4	96.0	108.4	123.7	169.7	195.2	156.7	165.4	158.9	129.7	99.9	95.2	73.6	**1,608.9**	**1,682.4**

Sources: Relevant public laws, House Appropriation Committee tables on relevant appropriations acts, DOD budget justification material, DOD, Cumulative CW-01-Z, Cumulative (war obligations database), March and June 2014. DOD figures are split by operation based on obligations incurred for each operation for funds of each fiscal year; State Department/USAID figures reflect enacted levels, and budget justification material on allocations between operations; VA budget justification materials for each year.

Notes:

[a] Reflects June 2014 amended DOD request, excludes OIR. Totals may not add due to rounding.

In addition, departmental spokesmen argue that congressional reluctance to accept DOD- proposed compensation reforms and weapon system cancellations could create an additional "hole" of $70 billion in DOD's current five-year defense plan, which already exceeds sequester caps by about 4.4%. In both FY2014 and FY2015, the Administration has contended that the BCA limits for both defense and nondefense should be raised with additional savings achieved from tax and entitlement reform, proposals that have not been addressed by Congress.[42]

The OCO or emergency designation can be applied to all or only some accounts within an appropriation act. There is no single account for war funding in any agency. Generally, war funding is appropriated in regular appropriation accounts for incremental expenses associated with war activities or programs. For DOD, war funding designations has been provided in individual accounts in emergency supplemental, omnibus, or DOD Appropriation Acts for amounts that cover incremental or additional expenses related to deploying military personnel, conducting combat or train and assist operations, and supporting troops overseas.[43]

With BCA spending limits in place until FY2021, some believe that the definition of what constitutes war funding may continue to be applied broadly. For example, concerned about DOD's proposal to end funding for A-10 ground attack aircraft in its base budget, the House version of the FY2015 National Defense Authorization Act included $635 million in Title XV for OCO funding to retain A-10 aircraft.[44]

In a similar way, the State Department has requested emergency or OCO designations for some of the costs of diplomatic operations or USAID programs associated with Afghanistan and Iraq, such as the Diplomatic and Consular Programs or the Economic Support Fund. Congress has also created new accounts or spending caps to fund activities that do not fit neatly into the purposes of regular accounts and to provide additional flexibility (see **Figure 9**).

Congressional Concerns

Recently, some Members have expressed concerns about and taken action to limit the tendency by both the Administration and Congress to apply the OCO designation to activities only tangentially related to war. For example, in H.R. 4435, the FY2015 National Defense Authorization Act, the House adopted the Mulvaney amendment to require that the Administration's requests comply with OMB's relatively strict 2010 war spending criteria that are intended to limit DOD war spending to activities and programs directly related to the incremental costs of war operations.[45] This provision would not apply to congressional decisions to attach an OCO designation to activities and programs that may be marginally related to those costs.

The FY2015 House Budget Resolution report contends that the OCO designation for war costs "has created a loophole that could be used to circumvent discretionary spending limits" and warns that "the Budget committee will be vigilant that the OCO/GWOT cap adjustment is not abused as a means of evading the statutory caps on discretionary spending."[46] During a July 17, 2014, hearing by the House Budget Committee on the FY2015 OCO request, both Democratic and Republican members raised concerns about ever-broader definitions of war costs. For example, ranking member Congressman Chris Van Hollen noted a tendency for

> creeping allocations from the base budget into the OCO budget. And I have to say, this is not just on the side of the administration. In fact, I think if you look at the record, Congress has actually been a greater offender in this area. But the reality is we have to work together—the executive branch, the congressional branch—to make sure that we have clear and transparent budgeting.[47]

In a similar vein, Congressman Bill Pascrell emphasized

> it's important that the committee ensure that the caps on spending in that law are respected or renegotiated. No one is innocent here. The administration, the Congress have used the OCO budget in the past to skirt the Budget Control Act's caps ... But it's critical that emergency spending be just that. For emergencies. And not just an accounting gimmick that undermines the budget discipline we've all agreed on.[48]

While acknowledging that BCA budget limits have made DOD planning "complicated and difficult," Congressman Adam Smith suggested that "a substantial portion of this OCO request really is not directly related to the war in Afghanistan [and] has been spread out amongst a variety of different other funds." [49] DOD witness Deputy Secretary Robert Work agreed that

> there's is an awful lot in this request that is outside Afghanistan, but that supports Afghanistan or is an integral part of our operations in Afghanistan. But I'd also like to make the point that as sequester has

> impacted the department, it has really squeezed our ability to absorb within the department unanticipated operations.[50]

While House Armed Services Committee Chairman, Bud McKeon called for a more expansive definition of war costs to cover "readiness shortfalls" developed over "a decade of war," Deputy Joint Chiefs of Staff, Admiral Winnefeld, responded that

> Mr. Chairman, in trying to stay true and faithful to what the concept of overseas contingency operations really means, we didn't view that kind of [full-spectrum] training necessarily as falling into that category. It'd be tempting to do that. We'd love to do that. But we really wanted to stay faithful and really reset this OCO idea into what it really is supposed to be.[51]

With the prospect of smaller war budgets as U.S. troop levels fall and as BCA caps continue through FY2021, Congress is likely to continue to face the question of what is appropriately designated as emergency or OCO.

The two key questions in assessing the use of emergency or "OCO" designations are:

- What is necessary for funding to qualify as "emergency" or "Overseas Contingency Operations" that exempts it from budget caps?
- How are war costs defined by the Administration, DOD, and the State Department?

Designating Funding As Emergency or OCO

Current budgetary law provides that any funding *designated* by Congress in statute and by the President in writing as "emergency" or "Overseas Contingency Operations" does not count against budget caps. In other words, what qualifies as "emergency" or "OCO" funding is its designation by Congress and the President.

The Chairs of the respective budget committees are required to raise budget limits to accommodate that spending, which effectively exempts that funding from spending limits set in either annual budget resolutions or more recently, the BCA (see **Box B.**).[52]

According to budget law, "emergency" spending is to be "unanticipated," meaning that it is "sudden ... urgent ... unforeseen ... and temporary" (See § 102 (4) (20) in **Box B.**). Although a Member can raise a point-of-order challenge to the emergency designation on the Senate floor, the challenge would have to be sustained by 60 votes, which has has seldom happened.[53]

Box B. Designating Funds as Emergency or for Overseas Contingency Operations: Budget Control Act of 2011 (Italics Added)

SEC. 251. (b) (2)(A) **ENFORCING DISCRETIONARY SPENDING LIMITS**

(b) ADJUSTMENTS TO DISCRETIONARY SPENDING LIMITS.—

(1) CONCEPTS AND DEFINITIONS.—When the President submits the budget under section 1105 of title 31, United States Code, OMB shall calculate and the budget shall include *adjustments to discretionary spending limits (and those limits as cumulatively adjusted) for the budget year and each outyear to reflect changes in concepts and definitions.* Such changes shall equal the baseline levels of new budget authority and outlays using up-to-date concepts and definitions, minus those levels using the concepts and definitions in effect before such changes. Such changes may only be made after consultation with the Committees on Appropriations and the Budget of the House of Representatives and the Senate, and that consultation shall include written communication to such committees that affords such committees the opportunity to comment before official action is taken with respect to such changes.

(2) SEQUESTRATION REPORTS.—When OMB submits a sequestration report under section 254(e), (f), or (g) for a fiscal year, OMB shall calculate, and the sequestration report and subsequent budgets submitted by the President under section 1105(a) of title 31, United States Code, shall include adjustments to discretionary spending limits (and those limits as adjusted) for the fiscal year and each succeeding year, as follows:

(A) ***EMERGENCY APPROPRIATIONS; OVERSEAS CONTINGENCY*** **OPERATIONS/GLOBAL WAR ON TERRORISM.**—If, for any fiscal year, appropriations for discretionary accounts are enacted that—

(i) *the Congress designates as emergency requirements in statute on an account by account basis and the President subsequently so designates*, or

(ii) *the Congress designates for Overseas Contingency Operations/Global War on Terrorism in statute on an account by account basis and the President subsequently so designates*, the adjustment shall be the total of such appropriations in discretionary accounts designated as emergency requirements or for Overseas Contingency Operations/Global War on Terrorism, as applicable."

Definitions of Emergencies

SEC. 251. ENFORCING DISCRETIONARY SPENDING LIMITS

(c) DISCRETIONARY SPENDING LIMIT

SEC. 102. DEFINITIONS

(20)The *term 'emergency' means* a situation that—''(A) requires new budget authority and outlays (or new budget authority and the outlays flowing therefrom) for the prevention or mitigation of, or response to, loss of life or property, or a threat to national security; and

(B) is *unanticipated.*

(21)The term 'unanticipated' means that the underlying situation is—

(A) *sudden*, which means quickly coming into being or not building up over time;

(B) *urgent*, which means a pressing and compelling need requiring immediate action;

(C) *unforeseen*, which means not predicted or anticipated as an emerging need; and

(D) *temporary*, which means not of a permanent duration.

The OCO designation was added in the Budget Control Act (P.L. 112-25), presumably to provide Congress with an alternate way to designate war funding than the "emergency" designation, which no longer seemed appropriate after over ten years of wars.[54] There are no criteria for the OCO designation nor is there a similar point of order to challenge it (**Box B.**).

In the initial years of the Afghan and Iraq wars, most war-related funding was provided in supplemental emergency appropriations. Starting in FY2004, DOD received some of its war funding in Title IX of its regular appropriation act to ensure that war funding was available at the beginning of the fiscal year but these funds were also designated as emergency; this funding was thus exempt from budget limits. DOD monies were first designated as "OCO" in FY2012 and also were exempt. When war funding needs were higher than anticipated, the Administration submitted additional emergency or OCO supplemental requests.[55]

CHANGES IN DOD DEFINITIONS OF WAR FUNDING

DOD definitions of what constitutes war-related activities and expenses have shifted over the years. Because of the flexibility of the emergency or OCO designations, some have questioned whether there are any limitations on what could be counted as war funding. The only check on the amount of funding that can be designated as either "emergency" or "OCO" is the requirement that Congress and the Administration agree.

Shifts in DOD definitions have reflected differing viewpoints about the extent, nature, and duration of the Afghan and Iraq wars and the "Global War on Terror" (GWOT) as well as growing budget pressures. Over the years, both Congress and the President have adopted sometimes more and sometimes less expansive definitions to accommodate the needs and pressures of the moment.

DOD's Regulations on War Funding

DOD's financial management regulations appear to specify fairly clearly the types of activities that would be considered related to contingency operations. Since the 1990s Bosnian war, DOD regulations have defined war costs as those expenses necessary to cover *incremental costs "that would not have been incurred had the contingency operation not been supported* (italics added)."[56]War costs would not cover, for example, base pay for troops or normal training activities since those are normal peacetime expenses, or planned equipment modernization.

Only those *costs in addition* to DOD's normal peacetime activities such as those *incurred because troops are deployed for war are to be considered OCO.* To identify these activities, the guidance requires that the services show how additional wartime deployments and operations affect peacetime assumptions about troop levels and operational tempo. Investment costs were only to be included if "necessary to support a contingency operation." [57]

War Expenses within Regular Accounts

Under these regulations, the following types of expenses were considered war costs:

- Military personnel funds to cover special pay for deployed personnel (e.g., imminent danger and separation pay) and the additional cost of activating reservists to full-time status;
- Operation and Maintenance (O&M) funds to transport troops and their equipment to Iraq and Afghanistan, conduct military operations, provide in-country support at bases, provide medical services for deployed troops, and repair and return war- worn equipment;
- Procurement funding to buy new weapons systems to replace war losses;
- Research, Development, Test & Evaluation (RDT&E) funds to develop more effective ways to combat war threats such as improvised explosive devices (IEDs) or roadside bombs;
- Working Capital Funds to expand inventories of spare parts and fuel to ensure wartime support;
- Military construction for facilities in bases in Iraq or Afghanistan or neighboring countries; and
- National and military intelligence (NIP and MIP) activities to gather and analyze war-related intelligence collected through surveillance and reconnaissance.

Additional Special Purpose Accounts

In addition, the Administration initiated several programs and accounts designed to fund specific war-related activities that do not fit into traditional accounts. These programs and accounts include:

- the Afghan Security Forces Fund (ASFF) and the Iraq Security Forces Fund (ISFF) to pay the cost of training, equipping and expanding the size of the Afghan and Iraqi armies and police forces;

- coalition support to reimburse regional allies (primarily Pakistan) for logistical costs of conducting counter-terror operations supporting U.S. efforts;
- the Commanders Emergency Response Program (CERP) to give individual commanders funds for small reconstruction projects and to pay local militias in Iraq and Afghanistan to gain support from local populations and counter- insurgent groups;
- the Afghan Infrastructure Fund (AIF) to finance larger reconstruction projects than under the CERP program and the Task Force for Business Stability Operations (TFBSO) to support privately-funded reconstruction activities;
- Joint Improvised Explosive Device (IEDs) Defeat Fund to develop, buy, and deploy new devices to improve force protection for soldiers against roadside bombs or IEDs; and
- Mine Resistant Ambush Protected (MRAP), Rapid Equipping Force, and Urgent Operational Needs Funds to Purchase Critical War Equipment Quickly.

Congressional Adds and DOD 'Must-Pay' Bills

As often occurs in supplemental appropriations, DOD added funds for unanticipated "must pay" bills and Congress added funds for programs that were designated as "emergency" or "OCO." For DOD, examples included unanticipated increases in basic housing allowances, incentive pays, fuel prices and base support expenses. Before the 9/11 attacks, such expenses would often be offset by reductions in other programs.

Congress added funds for childcare centers and barracks improvements to improve morale, post traumatic stress disorder (PTSD) and traumatic brain injury (TBI) as urgently-needed mental health programs, C-130 and C-17 transport aircraft facing production line cut-offs, and National Guard and Reserve equipment.

In recent years, Congress has transferred funds requested in base budget accounts to Title IX war- designated funding, ranging from monies for Mission and Other Operations funding training to base support of state-side facilities; in FY2014, Congress moved $9.2 billion in Operation and Maintenance funds requested in DOD's base budget to Title IX war funding.[58] The effect was to ease the limits of BCA spending caps.

DOD's 2006 Guidance Expands Definition of "War-Related"

In its initial July 19, 2006, guidance to the services for developing the FY2007 Supplemental and FY2008 war cost requests, DOD reiterated that war funding must comply with financial regulations limiting expenses to incremental costs or strictly war-related procurement. For example, this guidance specifically prohibited including the Army's modularity funds to reorganize units as war funding "because it is already programmed in FY2007 and the outyears," and warned that the services would have to demonstrate that investment items were "directly associated with GWOT operations," rather than to offset "normal recurring replacement of equipment."[59] In addition, the services would have to show that reset (the repair or replacement of war-worn equipment) plans were executable in FY2007, indicating it was urgently needed for war operations.

On October 25, 2006, however, Deputy Secretary of Defense Gordon England issued revised guidance for requesting war funds to the services that significantly changed these criteria. New requests were to be submitted within two weeks that reflected the "longer war on terror" rather than strictly the requirements for war operations in Iraq, Afghanistan and other counter-terror operations.[60] There was no definition of what types of expenses might be covered by the "longer war on terror." Presumably, this change reflected presidential policy. Since the longer war on terror was an integral part of DOD's national strategy, some might argue that these types of expenses would more appropriately be included in DOD's regular base budget, where they would compete with other defense needs.[61]

In response to this new guidance, the services expanded the types of programs and activities considered to be war-related. Examples included acceleration of planned equipment upgrades, modernization of the Army's Bradley fighting vehicles, M-1 tanks and its truck and vehicle fleet, and state-side base support. The effect of this policy change can be seen in the doubling of war-funded procurement from $22.9 billion in FY2006 to $49.5 billion in FY2007, with a peak of $65.9 billion in FY2009. The peak year also reflects a congressional decision to add $16.8 billion in a special account to quickly purchase mine resistant ambush protected (MRAP) vehicles, a heavy truck with a V-shaped hull that increased soldier survivability against roadside bombs or improvised explosive devices (IEDs) (**Table 7**).

Overall, between FY2001 and FY2014, DOD's war-designated procurement added almost $300 billion, or about 25%, to the $1.2 trillion in procurement funds appropriated to the base budget.[62] Although some war funding for procurement net was unanticipated, new wartime needs, such as uparmored Humvees for force protection, other war procurement funding converted Army brigades to modular units, and upgraded and purchased equipment sooner than planned.

For example, a 2007 CBO study found that more than 40% of the Army's spending for reset—the repair and replacement of war-worn equipment—was not for replacing lost equipment or repairing equipment sent home. Instead, Army funds were spent to upgrade systems to increase capability, to buy equipment to eliminate longstanding shortfalls in inventory, to convert new units to a modular configuration, and to replace equipment stored overseas for contingencies.[63]

Such investment funding contributed to DOD's modernization. In the case of the Army, particularly, war funding paid and accelerated the modernization of "nearly its entire fleet of ground combat vehicles [e.g., Abrams tanks and Bradley Infantry Fighting vehicles] and ... dramatically increased its stocks of small arms and support vehicles [e.g., Humvees, trucks]."[64] In this way, DOD war funding, in fact, financed some modernization requirements sooner than anticipated, effectively reducing funding that would otherwise be financed in DOD's base budget.

OMB 2009 Guidance Restores War Funding Limits

In 2009, at the beginning of the Obama administration, OMB issued new guidance outlining the criteria for war funding that largely restored earlier regulations. This guidance was modified in 2010 (**Appendix B**).

While the new OMB guidance restored some of the earlier limits on what would be considered "war-related" expenses, it adopted a broad geographic span for war-related activities. The theater of operations for "combat or direct combat support operations ... [for] non-classified war overseas contingency operations funding ... [is] to include Iraq, Afghanistan, Pakistan, Kazakhstan, Tajikistan, Kyrgyzstan, the Horn of Africa, Persian Gulf and Gulf nations, Arabian Sea, the Indian Ocean, the Philippines, and other countries on a case-by-case basis."[65] The criteria permitted the Administration to add other countries "on a case-by-case basis," as appears to be the case with the use of OCO funds for recent Syrian operations.

Under this new guidance, *procurement requirements* were limited to:

- war losses excluding items currently scheduled for replacement;
- upgrades directly supporting war operations; and
- put on contract *within 12 months*.

Operational requirements were confined to:

- transport to, from and within the theater of operations;
- *incremental costs to directly support operations with indirect costs to be evaluated on a case-by-case basis;* and
- fuel costs for plus "sufficient cash" to ensure combat operation.

War-related military construction was designed for

- the minimum to meet operational requirements; and
- "for temporary use" at non-enduring locations; with
- exceptions, on a case-by-case basis for construction at "enduring locations," tied to surge operations or major changes in operational requirements.

Certain items were *to be funded in the base budget rather than OCO (as had been the case):*

- regular training equipment,
- acceleration of upgrade programs,
- base closure projects,
- family support initiatives, childcare facilities, support for service members' spouses' professional development,
- recruiting and retention bonuses to maintain end-strength, and
- basic pay to maintain authorized end strength (italics added; see **Appendix B**).[66]

At the same time, then-Secretary of Defense Robert Gates pushed to move some war costs to the base budget that reflected long-term requirements for counter-terrorism operations, such as expanding special operations forces and higher funding for mental health. Some $8 billion was transferred from the war to the base budget in FY2010, and smaller amounts in FY2011.[67] DOD also included some funding for the Joint Improvised Explosive Device Defeat Fund (JIEDDF) in its base budget to cover research and procurement costs to counter IEDs or homemade land mines, with the rationale that this threat was likely to persist beyond the Afghan and Iraq wars. Congress, however, chose to move this funding to war-related Title IX of the DOD Appropriations Act.

Partly in response to this revised guidance, war procurement levels dropped from the peak of $65.9 billion in FY2008 to $34.6 billion in FY2009 to $32.6 billion in FY2010 and $29.8 billion in FY2011. Along with the new guidance, the end of U.S. combat operations and the withdrawals from Iraq and Afghanistan caused war procurement to fall to $16 billion in FY2012, $8 billion in FY2013, $7 billion in FY2014, and $6 billion in the FY2015 request (**Table 7**).

Force Structure and War Funding

Another area with shifting definitions of what is and what is not considered war funding are changes in force structure over the past decade. In FY2005 and FY2006, the Army requested and received $10 billion in war funding over two years to pay for the Army's ongoing modularity initiative to redesign and modernize its brigades. The Army claimed the initiative would extend the time between deployments ("dwell time"), which would reduce stress on those units that were frequently deployed. Studies by CBO and RAND questioned this conclusion, finding that modularity would only marginally improve rotation schedules.[68] DOD does not count modularity as a war cost (see **Table 6**).

The Army acknowledged that the distinction between war and base budget needs is murky "since modularity requirements mirror the equipment requirements the Army already procures for its units, the ability to precisely track modularity funds is lost."[69] Congress included the funds in the FY2005 and FY2006 war appropriations acts (effectively giving the Army more room in its regular budget for other things) but with the understanding that DOD would rely on the regular budget after FY2006 and set aside $25 billion in future years to cover these costs.[70]

The 2006 England guidance reversed this decision.[71] The FY2007 Supplemental included $3.6 billion to convert two Army brigade teams and create an additional Marine Corps regimental combat team, and the FY2008 war request included $1.6 billion to accelerate the creation of more modular brigades plus additional funds for equipping them (see "DOD's 2006 Guidance Expands Definition of "War-Related""").[72]

In addition to modularity, war funding was also used to pay for the cost to equip an additional 30,000 soldiers temporarily added to the Army in FY2004 to help reduce the frequency of wartime rotations for certain units. In January 2007 in light of war experience, DOD decided that Army and Marine Corps ground forces were needed for the long term and increased them by 92,000 from pre-war levels over the next several years so that the United States would be able to deploy substantial numbers of troops to conduct "stability operations" for prolonged periods of time.

The Army's pre-war level of 482,000 would increase by 65,000 in this "Grow the Army" initiative while the Marine Corps pre-war level of 175,000 would grow by 27,000 active-duty forces. The FY2007 Supplemental included $4.9 billion to cover the cost of 22,000 additional military personnel plus $1.7 billion for equipment and infrastructure although DOD promised that other funding for this force structure growth would be included in the regular budget starting in FY2009.[73]

In new strategic guidance issued in January 2012, after the death of Bin Laden and passage of the Budget Control Act mandating lower defense spending levels for the next decade, President Obama reversed this plan to size ground forces to conduct long-term stability operations, arguing instead that

> the United States will emphasize non-military means and military-to-military cooperation to address instability and reduce the demand for significant U.S. force commitments to stability operations ... [and that] U.S. forces will no longer be sized to conduct large-scale, prolonged stability operations.[74]

In 2013, as part of the changes to meet the first tranche of BCA reductions, the President announced that the size of the Army would be reduced from its wartime peak of 570,000 to 490,000 while the Marine Corps could be cut from 202,000 to 183,100—both close to pre-war levels. DOD then argued that the cost of gradually shedding Army and Marine Corps personnel because of this change should be considered a war cost, and included $6.0 billion in FY2013, $4.6 billion in FY2014, and $2.4 billion in FY2015 in its war request to cover the "over strength" or excess personnel on-board because of the change in strategic guidance.[75]

Unlike other war-related military expenses, this funding did not pay for troops deployed overseas in a war zone. Some may argue that these transition costs should be funded in the base budget since the decision reflected a choice about the appropriate size of all ground forces.

Reset Requirements

Another type of expense affected by the changing definitions of war funding is reset or reconstitution—the amount of funds needed to "reset" or restore the services' equipment to pre- war levels, the "process of bringing a unit back to full readiness once it has been rotated out of a combat operation."[76] Reset funds consist of both depot maintenance costs to repair equipment and replacement when repair is not worthwhile. Between FY2004 and FY2008, reset accounted for the largest increase, not only because ongoing operations had built up wear and tear on equipment, but also because of the 2006 Deputy Secretary of Defense England policy decision to broaden the definition of what was considered a war-related cost.[77]

Estimates of reset costs have changed frequently. In March 2005, CBO estimated that annual repair and replacement costs would run about $8 billion a year based on the current pace of operations and service data.[78] According to 2007 testimony by then-Army Chief of Staff, General Peter J. Schoomaker, and other military spokespeople, Army reset was estimated to be $12 billion to $13 billion a year as long as the conflict lasted at the current level and "for a minimum of two to three years beyond."[79]

There is some evidence that DOD front-loaded (funded in advance of need) its reset needs in 2007, a fact acknowledged by then-OMB Director Robert Portman in testimony at the time.[80] Congress has generally funded, if not added to, Army and Marine Corp reset requests.[81]The FY2007 Supplemental and the FY2008 war request both appear to include an extra year of Army and Marine Corps reset requirements; GAO has also questioned the accuracy of DOD's reset requirements.[82]

Another indication of frontloading reset is when procurement obligations rates are slower than normal (generally about 90% in the first year), resulting in large carryovers of war-related investment from earlier appropriations. As of the beginning of FY2008, for example, DOD had $45 billion in war-related carryover that had not been obligated or placed on contract.[83] As of April 30, 2010, about 40% of FY2009 war procurement funds remained unobligated.[84]

As mentioned, Army and Marine Corps spokesmen have also frequently predicted that reset funding would be needed two to three years after U.S. troops leave. Frontloading may reflect DOD desires to include reset funding before troop levels fall, anticipating greater difficulties in getting funding after U.S. troops leave. This frontloading practice may help explain why reset funding initially fell less rapidly than troop strength in Iraq but declined rapidly once all U.S. troops left.

In Iraq, reset funding halved from $16.5 billion in FY2009 to $8.5 billion in FY2010 while troop strength dropped one-third, perhaps reflecting the effects of the Iraq surge. In FY2011, the following year, reset funding remained at $8.9 billion while troop levels fell by another third. In FY2012 when troop levels fell to 9,200, Iraq reset funding fell steeply to $1.6 billion, then to $1.3 billion in FY2013 when troop levels in-country fell to zero. (**Table D-1**).

Reset funding for the Afghan war appears to lag troop reductions. Afghan reset funding decreased from $12.7 billion in FY2011 to $11.3 billion in FY2012 as troop strength dropped modestly from the 98,000 peak to 89,000, a decrease of close to 10% for both. By FY2013, however, with troop strength one-third below the peak, reset funding declined modestly to $9.9 billion. Despite another halving in troop strength between FY2013 and FY2014, reset decreased by $1.5 billion to $8.4 billion. And in the FY2015 request, Afghan troop funds increased to $9.2 billion while troop strength fell to 11,660 (**Table D-1**). This pattern could suggest frontloading of reset requests.

Over the war years, reset funding to repair, upgrade, and replace war-worn equipment contributed to both DOD's modernization and depot maintenance requirements for its equipment inventory. This war funding effectively filled some of DOD's base budget requirements by repairing and replacing equipment sooner than anticipated, potentially cushioning flattening and decreases in DOD budgets in recent years.

Military Construction and Permanent Bases

The scope of military construction raised concerns with some policy makers about whether extensive construction indicated DOD intentions to set up permanent U.S. bases in Iraq and in Afghanistan. Because of that concern, both defense appropriation and authorization acts include provisions that prohibit the United States from establishing permanent bases in either Iraq or Afghanistan.[85]

Over the past decade of war, DOD built up an extensive infrastructure to support troops and equipment in and around Iraq and Afghanistan. Military construction funding for this purpose more than doubled from $0.5 billion in FY2005 to a peak of $4.2 billion in FY2008,then dropped to zero in FY2012 (**Table 7**). In response to congressional concerns, DOD guidelines re-emphasized building that was "re-locatable" rather than permanent in Iraq and Afghanistan though some construction could be classified both ways. With the

U.S. withdrawals from Iraq and Afghanistan, bases have been either returned to the host country or demolished.[86]

DOD's Definition of "Other" Funding

In its monthly war cost tracking, DOD, lists "non-war" costs, including "must-pay" bills, modularity, and congressional additions and transfers. DOD does not include "excess over strength" as a non-war cost though some observers would count that as well.

Based on DOD's definition, "non-war" costs between FY2001 and FY2014 totaled $70.9 billion (**Table 6**). This total reflects growth from $6.6 billion in FY2005 to a peak of $12.1 billion in FY2008, dropping from $5 billion to $7 billion for FY2009 through FY2013, and then rising again to $10 billion in FY2014.[87] The amount of "non-war" costs could be considered higher than shown by DOD depending on definitions.

Assessing DOD's FY2015 War Request

DOD's initial FY2015 war request submitted in February 2014 was a "placeholder" figure because the President had not yet decided about the pace of future withdrawal of U.S. troops from Afghanistan. In June 2014, DOD submitted a specific FY2015 request for $58.6 billion for the Afghan war and post-war Iraq activities reflecting two policy announcements by President Obama about U.S. withdrawal plans.

Table 6. DOD's Non-War Costs, FY2001-FY2015

In Billions of Dollars	
Category	**Total, FY2001-FY2014**
Modularity	10.0
Fuel - Non-War	9.5
Other Non-War	51.4
TOTAL	70.9

Sources: DOD data provided to CRS and Cost of War Report, June 2014.

Notes: Includes costs that DOD does not track as war obligations except for war-related "non-DOD" intelligence, or National Intelligence Program programs, which are under the jurisdiction of the Director of National Intelligence.

In his February 2013 State of the Union address, the President announced that U.S. troops in Afghanistan would decrease to 33,000 by February of 2014, and that by the end of 2014, "our war in Afghanistan will be over," with later activities focusing "on two missions—training and equipping Afghan forces so that the country does not again slip into chaos, and counterterrorism efforts that allow us to pursue the remnants of al Qaeda and their affiliates."[88]

On May 27, 2014, President Obama announced further reductions in the number of U.S. troops in Afghanistan during the transition to an "advise and assist" role with decreases from

- 33,000 in February 2014 to 9,800 by January 1, 2015;
- by another halving to about 4,900 by the January 1, 2016; and
- the number of U.S. troops in Afghanistan would be an "embassy presence," of about 1,000 according to press reports by January 1, 2017.[89]

Recent press reports suggest that the decrease to 9,800 U.S. troops may be delayed from January 1, 2015, to at least the spring of 2015 as U.S. troops fill the "train and assist" role of some allied nations who are still finalizing their contributions. [90] Another pressure to retain more U.S. troop could also be posed by the recent decision by President Obama to allow DOD to provide more extensive support for Afghan operations through air support and sometimes accompanying Afghan troops on ground operations.[91]

These figures do not include over 60,000 U.S. troops located primarily in the region who provide "in-theater" support to war operations as well as headquarters and presence (**Figure 2** and **Appendix A**). The size of a U.S. "enduring presence" in the region after the withdrawal from Afghanistan remains a key policy question to be decided with significant cost implications.

DOD's FY2015 war request is $26.6 billion, or 31% below the FY2014 enacted level, while troop strength in Afghanistan falls by 69%[92] (**Table 7**). In testimony before the House Armed Services Committee, Department of Defense Comptroller, Mike McCord, stated that the decrease in FY2015's request reflects "a continued downward trajectory of our war-related spending as we conclude our combat mission in Afghanistan after 13 years of war ..." but argues that DOD is also "faced with covering the costs of returning, repairing and replacing equipment ... [and] the costs associated with our broader presence in the Middle East, from which we support a number of critical missions in-country from FY2014 to FY2015."[93]

Table 7. DOD Funding for OEF and OIF/OND, FY2001-FY2015 Request by Title

In Billions of Dollars and Percent Change														
Fiscal Year	By Title in Billions of Dollars of Budget Authority (BA)										Annual Change in War Funding and Average Troop Strength In-Country			
	Mil.Pers.	O&M	Rev.Fds	Proc.	RDT&E	Mil.Con.	Fam.Hsg.	CTPF[a]	ERI[a]	Resc.[b]	Total in $ Bs	In-Cntry Troops in 000s	% Annual Chge in $Bs	% Annual Chge in Stgth
2001	0.0	21.8	0.0	1.2	0.0	0.0	0.0	0.0	0.0	na	$22.9	na	na	na
2002	0.2	15.4	0.0	1.2	0.0	0.1	0.0	0.0	0.0	na	$16.9	5.2	-26%	na
2003	15.0	52.8	0.0	3.7	0.8	0.2	0.0	0.0	0.0	na	$72.5	78.1	330%	1391%
2004	19.1	61.8	2.1	6.9	0.3	0.5	0.0	0.0	0.0	na	$90.8	145.8	25%	87%
2005	17.4	37.5	1.5	17.4	0.6	1.1	0.0	0.0	0.0	na	$75.6	161.0	-17%	10%
2006	16.5	72.4	3.0	22.9	0.8	0.2	0.0	0.0	0.0	na	$115.8	159.1	53%	-1%
2007	18.9	93.6	1.1	49.5	1.5	1.7	0.0	0.0	0.0	na	$166.3	181.5	44%	14%
2008	19.1	93.3	2.7	65.9	1.6	4.2	0.0	0.0	0.0	na	$186.9	186.6	12%	3%
2009	19.9	87.3	0.9	34.6	0.3	2.7	0.0	0.0	0.0	na	$145.7	184.0	-22%	-1%
2010	16.9	108.3	1.5	32.6	1.0	2.0	0.0	0.0	0.0	na	$162.4	175.8	11%	-4%
2011	15.6	110.2	0.5	29.8	1.4	1.2	0.0	0.0	0.0	na	$158.8	144.9	-2%	-18%
2012	11.3	86.8	0.4	16.1	0.5	0.0	0.0	0.0	0.0	na	$115.1	95.8	-28%	-34%
2013	12.1	61.5	0.0	8.1	0.2	0.0	0.0	0.0	0.0	na	$82.0	63.4	-29%	-34%

Table 7. (Continued)

In Billions of Dollars and Percent Change														
Fiscal Year	By Title in Billions of Dollars of Budget Authority (BA)										Annual Change in War Funding and Average Troop Strength In-Country			
	Mil.Pers.	O&M	Rev.Fds	Proc.	RDT&E	Mil.Con.	Fam.Hsg.	CTPF[a]	ERI[a]	Resc.[b]	Total in $ Bs	In-Cntry Troops in 000s	% Annual Chge in $Bs	% Annual Chge in Stgth
2014	8.1	69.7	0.3	7.0	0.1	0.0	0.0	0.0	0.0	na	$85.2	37.2	4%	-41%
2015 Req.[c]	5.5	42.1	0.1	6.0	0.1	0.0	0.0	4.0	0.9	-0.1	$58.6	11.7	-31%	-69%
House Passed[d]	5.1	60.1	0.0	14.2	0.0	0.0	0.0	0.0	0.0	0	$79.40	11.7	-7%	-69%
Senate Repted[e]	5.4	43.1	0.1	7.2	0.1	0.0	0.0	1.0	-0.6	-0.6	$58.90	11.7	-31%	-69%
Enacted, 2001-FY2014														
Title	190.2	972.4	14.1	296.8	9.2	14.0	0.0	0.0	0.0	na	$1,496.80	na	na	na
Total w/ FY2015 Req.														
Title	195.6	1014.5	14.2	302.9	9.3	14.1	0	0.9	-0.1	-0.1	$1,555.40	na	na	na

Sources: CRS calculations based on Table 2-1 in Department of Defense, Office of the Under Secretary of Defense (Comptroller), National Defense Budget Estimates for FY 2015, April 2014; http://comptroller.defense.gov/Portals/45/Documents/defbudget/

fy2015/FY15_Green_Book.pdf. Average strength calculated from DOD's monthly "Boots on the Ground" reports, 2001-June 2015; see **Appendix A**.

Notes:

a. Counterterrorism Partnership Fund (CTPF) and European Reassurance Initiative (ERI).

b. Rescissions are applied to relevant fiscal year after request and shown separately in requests.

c. Reflects Administration's amended June 2014 request.

d. H.R. 4870 as passed by the House reflects initial placeholder request.

e. H.R. 4870 as reported by the Senate Appropriations committee reflects Administration's amended June 2014 request.

In justifying both its FY2014 and FY2015 requests, DOD contended that war expenses would not fall proportionately with troop levels because the cost of closing bases; returning, repairing, or disposing of equipment; and maintaining some 60,000 troops in the region offset some of the lower cost of deploying fewer troops at lower operating tempo.[94] In addition, DOD Deputy Secretary Robert Work argued that costs remained high because of

> continued support for the Afghan national security forces, our coalition partners in theater, and pay for the retrograde equipment and personnel will continue to reset the forces to enable a truly vast range of support activities, including logistics, intelligence, and will support a portion of the temporary Army and Marine Corps in strength that supports OEF, which has been approved by Congress.[95]

The FY2015 DOD OCO request also includes $4 billion for DOD's Counterterrorism Partnership Fund (CTPF), a controversial, new transfer fund intended to provide "a flexible mechanism that allows the Department of Defense (DOD) and the Federal Government as a whole to respond more nimbly to evolving terrorist threats from South Asia to the Sahel." It also includes $925 million for a European Reassurance Fund (ERI) to "reassure allies of the U.S. commitment to their security and territorial integrity as members of the NATO Alliance" in response to Russian moves in the Ukraine.[96] (The Administration requests another $1 billion for the State Department's CTPF account.)

Some ways to evaluate DOD's FY2015 request for war funding which Congress may consider as part of the appropriations and authorization process may include:

- reviewing whether DOD has spent all the war funds appropriated over the past several years;
- comparing operational and troop costs experienced during the Iraq drawdown with the proposed FY2015 costs of the Afghanistan drawdown; and
- comparing the Administration's new CTPF proposal to expand funding for "Train and Equip" counterterrorism training programs with previous similar programs.

Passed in June 2014, the House-passed version of the DOD Appropriations bill, H.R. 4870, reflected the Administration's initial OCO placeholder request, while the Senate-reported version of H.R. 4870 marked up DOD's amended request.

Neither the House nor the Senate version includes the additional $5.5 billion requested for DOD in November 2014 to combat the Islamic State by conducting air strikes in Syria and Iraq and re- instituting training of Iraqi security forces. That request is discussed separately below because the request is for a new military operation with different purposes ("The New Request to Counter the Islamic State").

Has DOD Used All Its War Funds?

One standard measure to evaluate whether the budget authority (BA) appropriated is sufficient or in excess of the amount needed is to examine an agency's previous obligations history (obligations reflect when contracts to purchase goods or services are signed and when military and civilian personnel are paid). If funds are not obligated within their specified life, they are presumably not needed during that time. The funds then lapse and are returned to the Treasury, and reduce the deficit.[97]

Funds to cover day-to-day expenses and activities like military personnel and Operation and Maintenance (O&M) funds are available for one year, while procurement monies to buy weapon systems are available for three years because the contracting process takes more time. [98] As contracts are executed, funds are then disbursed.

Amounts designated for war (as emergency or OCO) are specified in Title XV of the defense authorization and Title IX of the DOD appropriation acts. These funds are separately tracked by DOD in its accounting systems, and reported to Congress. DOD has some flexibility to move funds from base budget accounts to those designated for war. DOD can also transfer funds from one emergency or OCO-designated account to other war-designated accounts. If funds are inadequate, DOD can transfer funds from base budget accounts to emergency or OCO-designated accounts, also within caps set in law.[99]

Using DOD sources, CRS analyzed DOD's obligations of war funds appropriated between FY2008 and FY2014 to see how much of that funding lapsed after its life expired, and the amounts that DOD transferred from the base budget to meet war needs because war funding was inadequate.

Lapsed War Funds

Between FY2008 and FY2013, a total of $17.2 billion in funds designated for war lapsed. The amount of war funding that lapsed made up 2.3% of the total available. At the same time, DOD transferred a total of $9.8 billion from its base budget funding to meet war needs or 0.9% share of available war funds (**Table 8**). In terms of dollar amounts, lapsed funding ranged from a low of $1.2 billion in FY2009 to a high of $5.8 billion in FY2010. The largest dollar amount of lapsed funds came from one-year monies for military personnel and O&M, while the highest shares of lapsed funding came from three-five year funds primarily for procurement (**Figure 5**). There are other indications that war obligations in FY2014 may be more than needed. Based on DOD's June 2014 war cost report, some obligations are slower than the experience of the past five years. For example, while O&M, Army obligations averaged 65% as of June over the past five years, the share obligated in June, 2014 made up 60% of available BA (**Figure 6**). If obligations in the last quarter of FY2014 followed the pattern of the past five years, then O&M, Army obligations would total $22.7 billion out of $29.7 billion available. That would leave some $6.7 billion in available BA that could lapse unless DOD transferred the funds for other uses.[100]

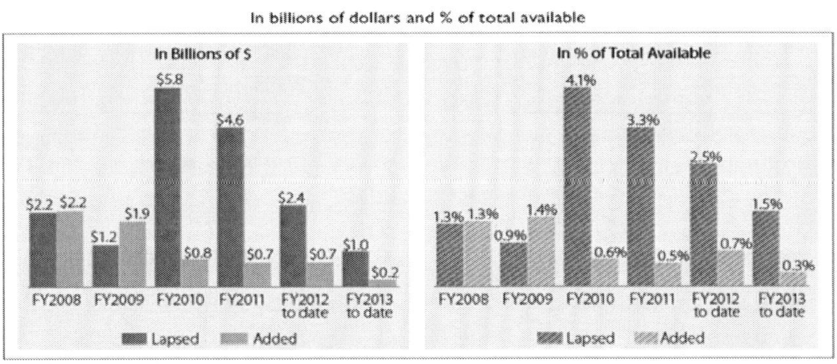

Source: CRS calculations based on tables in September reports for FY2008-FY2014 (as of June, 2014).

Notes: Lapsed funding reflects monies whose life has expired except to adjust signed contracts. Adjustments in later years generally reduce the amount obligated. For FY2012 and FY2013, DOD data is as of June 2014 and so lapsed funds only reflect monies with a one-year life. At this time, it is unknown whether FY2012 and FY2013 funds that are available for two or three years will be obligated before their life expires.

Figure 5.War Funding: Lapsed and Transferred.

Table 8. Execution of War Funding, FY2009-May FY2014

In Billions of Dollars and % of Total		
Status of War Funds	Cumulative Amount in Billions of $	As % of Total
Lapsed[a]	$17.2	2.3%
Added from base budget[b]	$9.8	0.9%

Source: CRS calculations based on DOD, Table, "Backup Material in Cost of War Execution Reports," September of 2009, 2010, 2011, 2012, and May 2014.

Notes:

a. For up to five years after the end of their statutory life, BA can be used to make adjustments to signed contracts; most adjustments reduce reported costs so lapsed amounts would be higher than shown here.

b. DOD can transfer funds appropriated for its base budget to war funding as needed.

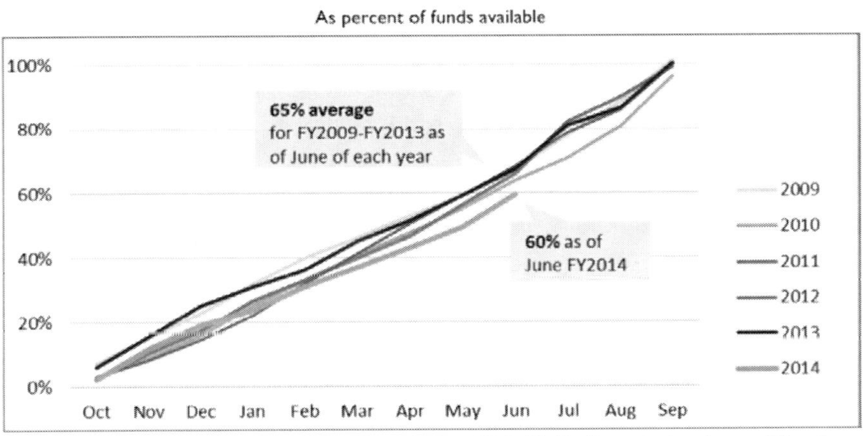

Source: CRS calculations based on Cumulative CW-01-Z, Cumulative [war obligations data base] as of June 2014.

Figure 6. O&M, Army Monthly Obligations, FY2009-FY2014.

FY2014 War Funds Finance Airstrikes, Ebola Emergency, and Aircraft

In August and September 2014, DOD submitted three requests to the four congressional defense committees to transfer a total of $2.66 billion in FY2014 O&M, Army war funds to pay for other expenses:

- $165 million in unanticipated expenses of conducting airstrikes against the Islamic State (IS) in Iraq and Syria;

- $1.0 billion to provide humanitarian assistance for the Ebola crisis in several nations in West Africa; and
- $1.5 billion to finance buys of Joint Strike Fighters and AH-64 helicopters to replace war losses.

Transfer provisions require that war funds can only be used to finance other more urgent war needs. In all three cases, the funds transferred were to be used for other OCO needs, including the Ebola response, which was "deemed" an OCO requirement.[101]

DOD received congressional approval to transfer O&M, Army funds to pay for the Navy's additional aviation fuel and maintenance for ships deployed to support Navy airstrikes in Iraq and Syria in the Middle East as well as the cost of replacing Hellfire missiles. To finance this unanticipated expense, DOD tapped O&M, Army monies that were not needed because aviation units deployed in Central Command to support Afghanistan were sent home sooner than anticipated.

DOD also received approval to provide $750 million in humanitarian assistance for the Ebola crisis, using additional O&M, Army funds that were available because of lower support costs for units re-deployed home sooner than planned.[102]

DOD also asked to transfer an additional $1.5 billion from O&M, Army war funds not needed because re-deployments occurred earlier than planned to finance the purchase of:

- 21 AH-64 helicopters to replace 21 OH-58F helicopters lost in 2012;
- 6 F-35 Joint Strike Fighters (JSF) to replace 6 AV-8Bs lost in 2012; and
- 2 JSFs to replace two F-15 aircraft lost in 2012-2013. [103]

Congress denied these requests because the replacement purchases were already included in DOD's future budget plans, violating one of the OMB criteria for war funding (see "OMB 2009 Guidance Restores War Funding Limits" and **Appendix B**).[104]

War Funds Cut during the FY2013 Sequester

Another potential indicator of previous excess war funding is DOD's implementation of the FY2013 sequester that was levied on all accounts, both base and war.[105] In January 2013, before the March sequester order, Deputy Secretary Ashton Carter issued guidance to the services to "fully protect all wartime operations," and "protect investments funded in Overseas Contingency Operations if associated with urgent operational needs."[106] In May 2013, Secretary of Defense Chuck Hagel warned that "because our wartime budget is also subject to sequestration, we must utilize funds originally budgeted for other purposes in order to provide our troops at war with every resource they need."[107]

Under sequester rules, DOD's individual accounts for O&M funds and individual weapon system programs must be cut by the amounts specified in the OMB order. Because both base and OCO funds are generally in the same accounts, DOD has the flexibility to allocate sequester reductions to base or OCO-designated funds as long as the overall sequester savings are achieved. So, DOD could have assigned all of the sequester cuts to base accounts to protect war funding.

Instead, DOD directed $5.3 billion of its total sequester cut of $37.2 billion to war funding, a proportional share with both base and OCO funding cut by 6%. OCO-designated O&M accounts were cut by 6% and OCO-designated procurement funds by10%.[108] DOD may have believed that OCO-designated funds could absorb these cuts without jeopardizing war operations.

Changes in Per-Troop Costs

Another metric that might be used to assess DOD requests is to examine the cost per troop over time. Conceptually, per-troop costs would be expected to decrease with higher troop levels, reflecting economies of scale. This has generally not been the case in Iraq and Afghanistan.

As the number of troops decrease during withdrawals, per-troop costs would be expected to rise temporarily because support costs remain high as bases stay open to support remaining troops, and because one-time costs must be paid to close bases, ship home and repair equipment retained in-theater, and dispose of equipment.[109] Although per-troop costs increased in both Iraq and Afghanistan during withdrawals, the increase has been steeper in Afghanistan (**Figure 7**).

At the same time, such increases could be at least partially offset by lower costs to support fewer U.S. troops and conduct the less-costly train-and-assist mission.[110]

To capture costs likely to rise or fall with troop strength, CRS defined per-troop costs as

- operational costs to conduct combat operations and support deployed troops;
- investment for war-related procurement, RDT&E, and military construction; and
- excluding special purpose, flexible accounts such as training Afghan and Iraq security forces, which would not necessarily change with deployed troop strength.

In Iraq and in Afghanistan

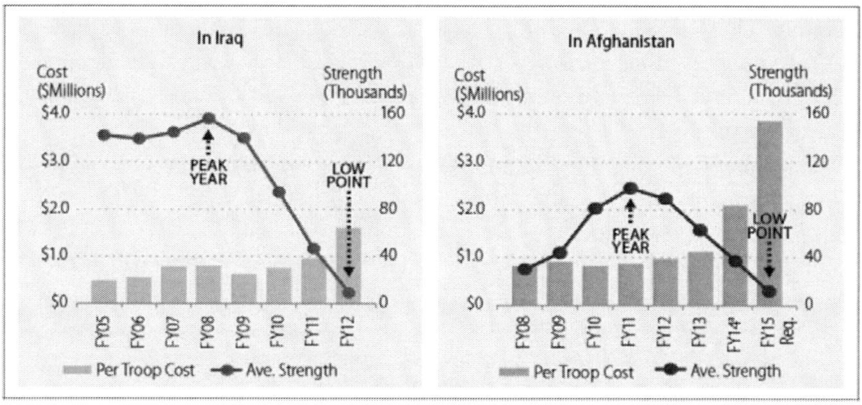

Sources: CRS calculated average strength from DOD's monthly "Boots on the Ground" reports, and operational costs from DOD's Cost of War reports. Operational costs include war-designated military personnel and operation and maintenance obligations excluding funds to train Afghan and Iraq security forces, coalition support and other flexible funds set up to meet special war needs; investment costs include war- designated procurement, RDT&E and military construction from DOD's monthly Cost of War reports.

Figure 7. Changes in Per-Troop Cost before and after Withdrawals.

Per-Troop Costs Rise with Troop Levels

The cost per deployed troop—operational and investment—rose from $490,000 in FY2005 to $800,000 in FY2008 in Iraq, a 63% increase. During the same period, the per-troop cost in Afghanistan rose from $580,000 in FY2005 to $820,000 in FY2008, a 41% increase (**Figure 7**). When the cost per troop rises substantially, questions may be raised about the reasons.

A variety of factors may help explain increases in per-troop costs, including:

- rising intensity of operating tempo;
- unanticipated need for more force protection (e.g., armored Humvees);
- growth in base support facilities for soldiers in-country and in the region;
- higher command, communications, control, computers and intelligence support;
- expanded war-related benefits;
- cumulative effects of war usage on equipment;
- DOD policy decisions to expand the definition of war costs (see section on "DOD's 2006 Guidance Expands Definition of "War-Related""); and
- deficient wartime contracting practices and corruption in DOD's purchase of war-time goods and services.[111]

Increases during Withdrawals

Per-troop costs increased more steeply during U.S. withdrawal from Iraq and Afghanistan than during other phases of the operations. In Iraq, per-troop costs doubled from $800,000 in FY2008 to $1.6 million in FY2012 when the last U.S. troops left the country. In Afghanistan, per-troop costs fluctuated between $820,000 and $910,000 between FY2008 and FY2011. Based on the FY2015 request, per-troop costs in Afghanistan are to increase by 345% or over three-fold from $870,000 in FY2011 to $3.9 million in FY2015. This growth in Afghanistan is steeper than in Iraq in terms of both dollars and rate of increase (**Figure 7**).

In previous years, Congress has reduced DOD's request based on similar analysis of trends in per- troop costs. For example, in FY2011, Congress transferred over $5 billion to the Overseas Contingency Operations Transfer Fund (OCOTF) after the House Appropriations report found excessive growth, and in FY2013 war appropriation, Army Operation and Maintenance was cut by $500 million because of "unjustified growth in average operations per troop."[112]

DOD Drawdown Costs in Iraq and Afghanistan

Another way to gauge the funding in the FY2015 war funding request is to compare the withdrawal experiences in both countries for operational and investment costs separately.[113] The trends described below suggest that DOD's FY2015 request for operational expenses in Afghanistan may be higher than would be expected in light of the experience during the Iraq withdrawal.

Changes in Troop Strength in Iraq and Afghanistan in Earlier Years

Between FY2005 and FY2008, troop strength in Iraq rose gradually from 143,000 to 157,000, a 10% increase. From FY2005 to FY2009, troop strength in Afghanistan more than doubled from 18,000 to 43,800, a more rapid increase than in Iraq.

In Iraq and in Afghanistan, FY2005-FY2015 Request

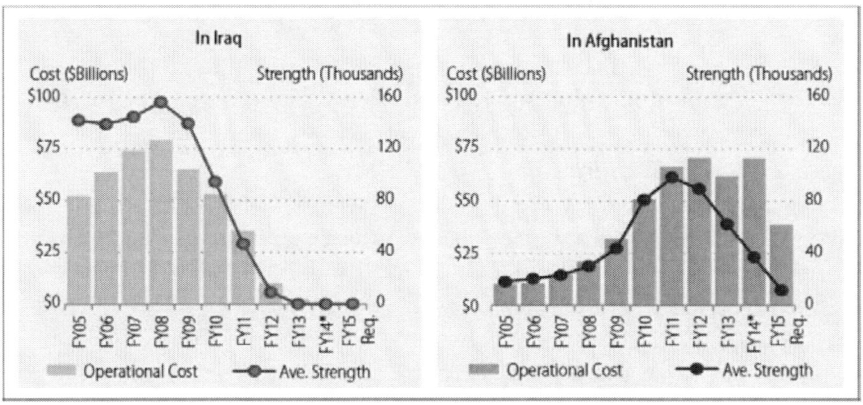

Sources: CRS calculated average strength from DOD's monthly "Boots on the Ground" reports, and operational costs from DOD's Cost of War reports. Operational costs include military personnel and operation and maintenance obligations excluding funds to train Afghan and Iraq security forces, coalition support, and other flexible funds set up to meet special war needs.

Figure 8. Changes in Troop Strength and Operational Costs.

The peak strength in Iraq was 156,000 during the surge in FY2008 while the peak strength in Afghanistan was 100,000 during the troop surge. In both countries, the rate of decrease from these peaks was similar.

Compared to the peak in FY2008, U.S. troop levels in Iraq dropped by

- about 10% to 140,000 in FY2009;
- one-third to 94,000 in FY2010;
- two-thirds to 47,000 in FY2011; and
- over 90% to 9,200 in FY2012 as all U.S. troops left Iraq.

The pace of the troop withdrawal in Afghanistan is similar to Iraq. Compared to the peak troop strength of 98,300 during the Afghan surge in FY2010, troop levels dropped by

- 9% to 90,000 in FY2012;
- about one-third to 63,000 in FY2013;
- almost two-thirds to 37,000 in FY2014; and
- almost 90% to 12,000 in FY2015 request.

So, in both operations, compared to peak strength during their respective troop surges, during their respective withdrawals, the number of U.S. troops initially declined gradually and then fell by roughly a third, two-thirds, and then 90% from the peak level before the final withdrawal (**Figure 8**).[114]

Comparing Operational Costs and Strength

Total operational costs in Iraq rose steadily while troop strength remained fairly stable.

At the same time, operational costs in Afghanistan closely mirrored changes in troop strength. In both cases, operating tempo rose before and during troop surges.

Both wars included fairly steep declines in troop strength from peak levels that occurred during FY2008 in Iraq and FY2011 in Afghanistan. While operational costs in Iraq declined proportionately, those in Afghanistan continued to rise sharply, showing a clear discrepancy between DOD's current FY2015 request and the Iraq experience (**Figure 8**).

Although operational costs in Afghanistan have generally exceeded those in Iraq because of the high costs of transportation and other logistical difficulties, these factors alone would not appear to explain the higher costs during the withdrawal in DOD's FY2015 request, given similarities in costs in both theaters in FY2009-2011.

Comparing Investment Costs and Troop Strength

Investment cost changed roughly in parallel with troop strength since FY2005 in both Iraq and Afghanistan. In earlier years, investment in Iraq grew sharply even as troop strength remained stable, presumably reflecting the new guidance from Deputy Secretary England redefining the scope of war costs as well as a buildup in repair and replacement costs (**Figure 9**).

Afghanistan's investment costs grew with troop strength after FY2009, and then remained roughly level between FY2009 and FY2011 even though strength grew. In both wars, investment spending declined fairly rapidly with troop strength, though more slowly in Afghanistan (**Figure 9**).

FLEXIBLE FUNDING AND THE NEW COUNTERTERRORISM PARTNERSHIP FUND (CTPF)

One of the more controversial issues in the FY2015 request is the Administration's proposal to set up the new Counterterrorism Partnership Fund (CTPF) intended to allow DOD and other agencies "to respond more nimbly to evolving terrorist threats from South Asia to the Sahel" by building "partnership capacity."[115]

DOD's CTPF is a $4 billion OCO-designated transfer account available for three years. Monies could be spent in any appropriation account, in any geographical location, for a variety of general purposes, and notwithstanding any other provision of law. The Administration argues that this broad flexibility is necessary. Budget justification materials provide nonbinding illustrative funding allocations and Congress could only participate in allocation decisions by raising objections after receiving notifications 15 days in advance of transferring funds.[116]

The CTPF has raised congressional concerns because of the amount requested and the flexibility to apply the funds for broadly-defined purposes after enactment, including an illustrative allocation of $500 million to train and equip Syrian opposition groups fighting the Islamic State (IS).

The Administration is also requesting funds for a less controversial new European reassurance initiative (ERI) to help "reassure NATO allies and bolster the security and capacity of U.S. partners" and counter recent Russian actions in the Ukraine for more specific activities such as increasing the number of bilateral and multilateral exercises in Europe, building partner capacity with newer Eastern European NATO members and expanding U.S. presence through additional pre-positioning of U.S. equipment.[117]

The issue for Congress is the amount of flexibility to give DOD to respond to needs that it cannot define when appropriations are requested. From the Administration's perspective, the trade-off is between flexibility and acting quickly. From a congressional perspective, the trade-off is between flexibility and congressional oversight.

Unlike individual appropriation accounts where funds are used for specific types of purposes and expenses, or specific items, flexible funding generally appropriates a lump sum or sets an overall cap on the amount of money that can be spent and then permits an agency to move the monies to different accounts for different purposes depending on how needs develop. To assess the CTPF proposal, CRS compared it with other flexible funds for war approved by Congress since the 9/11 attacks.

Rationales for Flexible Funding

Since the 9/11 attacks, Congress established 10 new, specific accounts and set a dozen new spending caps within other accounts to provide DOD with flexibility to conduct various war- related activities that do not neatly fit into traditional accounts that cover specific types of expenses (e.g., military personnel). Funding has either been provided in a lump sum or can be drawn from other accounts up to a certain cap. In some cases funds are available for a year and in others for more than one year, which enhances flexibility.

In Iraq and in Afghanistan, FY2005-FY2015 Request

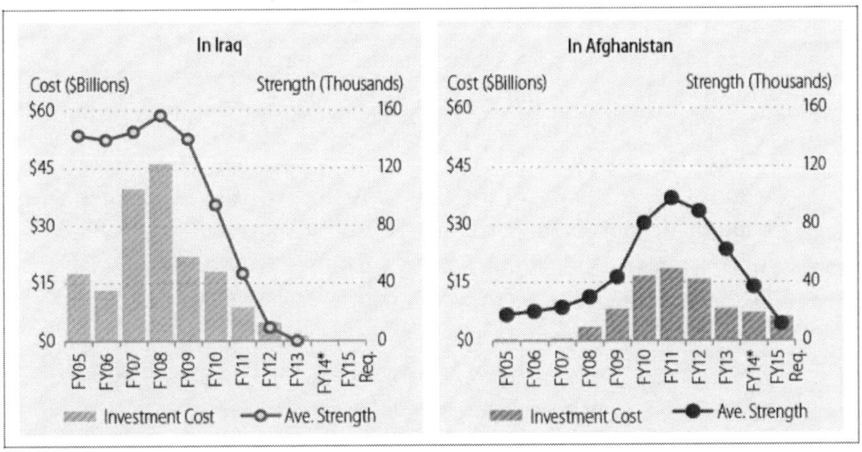

Sources: CRS calculated average strength from DOD's monthly "Boots on the Ground" reports, and investment costs (procurement, RDT&E, and military construction) from DOD's Cost of War reports.

Figure 9. Changes in Troop Strength and Investment Cost.

To establish the scope of the program, Congress generally defines purposes and criteria for use of the funds, countries eligible, types of security assistance provided, and notification before or after funds are obligated. Congress has typically revised Administration requests by reducing the funding amounts, narrowing flexibility, and requiring more detailed notification and reporting. In light of this history and congressional concerns, the Administration's FY2015 proposals for the Counterterrorism Partnership Fund (CTPF) and the European Reassurance Initiative (ER) may also be modified.

Flexible funds have played an important role in war funding, making up a significant share of total funding ranging from a high of 100% in FY2001 immediately after the 9/11 attacks to a low of 7% in FY2003. Between FY2005 and FY2014, flexible war funding fluctuated between 15% and 23% of total DOD war funding. After FY2008, the share of flexible funding enacted declined, presumably reflecting less uncertainty as war needs decline. The FY2015 DOD request reverses this trend, rising to 26% of war funding (**Table 9**).

Congress has approved these lump-sum flexible funds in the past 13 years to enable DOD to respond to different types of uncertainties in wartime operations and needs

- at the beginning of wars when expenses are not known;
- to expand DOD's Train and Equip authorities for partner nations or non-state actors before agreements have been reached;
- to provide for wartime activities, like training Afghan and Iraqi security forces, or reconstruction activities where expenses cut across traditional appropriation accounts;
- to meet unexpected urgent war-time requirements; and
- to move monies between accounts after enactment to deal with the unexpected.

Table 9. DOD'S Flexible Funds for War

Accounts/ Caps	2001	2002	2003	2004	2005	2006	2007	2008	2009	2010	2011	2012	2013	2014	2015 Req.	Total: FY2001-F2015
	In Billions of Dollars of Budget Authority															
	Early Stages of War															**68.558**
Defense Emergency Response Fund (DERF)*	22.934	15.296	0	0	0	0	0	0	0	0	0	0	0	0	0	38.230
Iraq Freedom Fund(IFF)*	0	0	15.678	1.988	3.800	4.659	0.406	3.797	0	0	0	0	0	0	0	30.328
Train and Equip: Emergency/OCO designated																**26.728**
Coalition Support spending cap	0	0	1.400	1.150	1.220	0.935	1.100	1.100	1.200	1.570	1.600	1.690	1.650	1.257	1.660	17.532
Pakistan Counterinsurgency Fund account	0	0	0	0	0	0	0	0	0.400	0	0.800	0	0	0	0	1.200
10 U.S.C. Sec. 127d Global Lift and Sustain cap	0	0	0	0	0	0	0	0.038	0.004	0.005	0.010	0.007	0.036	0.063	na	0.211
Afghanistan and Iraq Lift & Sustain, Sec. 1234, FY2008 NDAA as amended	0	0	0	0	0	0	0	.400	.400	.400	.400	.450	na	na	na	2.050

Table 9. (Continued)

In Billions of Dollars of Budget Authority																
Accounts/ Caps	2001	2002	2003	2004	2005	2006	2007	2008	2009	2010	2011	2012	2013	2014	2015 Req.	Total: FY2001-F2015
Afghanistan Lift & Sustain, Sec. 1216, FY2013 NDAA	0	0	0	0	0	0	0	0	0	0	0	0	.450	.450	.450	1.350
Sec. 1208 Support Foreign and Irregular Forces cap	0	0	0	0	0.025	0.025	0.025	0.025	0.025	0.04	0.045	0.05	0.05	0.05	0.05	0.410
Counterterrorism Partnership Fd (CTPF)	0	0	0	0	0	0	0	0	0	0	0	0	0	0	4.000	4.000
Train and Equip: Base Budget																**[4.254]**
Global Security Contingency Fund cap (DOD)	[0]	[0]	[0]	[0]	[0]	[0]	[0]	[0]	[0]	[0]	[0]	[0.200]	[.200]	[0.200]	[0.030]	[.630]
Sec. 1203 Build Counterterrorism Capacity in Yemen and African Nations cap	[0]	[0]	[0]	[0]	[0]	[0]	[0]	[0]	[0]	[0]	[0]	0	[.150]	[0.150]	[0.150]	[.450]

In Billions of Dollars of Budget Authority																
Accounts/ Caps	**2001**	**2002**	**2003**	**2004**	**2005**	**2006**	**2007**	**2008**	**2009**	**2010**	**2011**	**2012**	**2013**	**2014**	**2015 Req.**	**Total: FY2001-F2015**
Sec. 1206 Build capacity of Foreign Forces cap/Global Train & Equip	[0]	[0]	[0]	[0]	[0]	[0.200]	[0.300]	[0.300]	[0.350]	[0.350]	[0.350]	[0.350]	[.274]	[0.350]	[0.350]	[3.174]
Sec. 1208 Support Foreign Forces Diasarming Lord's Resistance Army cap	[0]	[0]	[0]	[0]	[0]	[0]	[0]	[0]	[0]	[0]	[0]	[.050]	[.050]	[.050]	[.050]	[.200]
Special War Needs: Training Afghan and Iraq Security Forces																**146.176**
Afghanistan Security Forces Fund (ASFF)	ns	ns	0	[.348]	1.285	1.908	7.406	2.750	5.607	9.167	11.619	10.200	5.124	4.727	4.109	63.902
Iraq Security Forces Fund Fd (ISFF)	ns	ns	0	[5.000]	5.700	3.007	5.542	3.000	1.000	1.500	1.500	0	0	0	0	21.249
Mine Resistant Ambush Protected (MRAP) Fund transfer account	0	0	0	0	0	0	0	16.83	6.243	7.404	3.415	2.2	0	0	0	36.092

Table 9. (Continued)

In Billions of Dollars of Budget Authority																
Accounts/ Caps	**2001**	**2002**	**2003**	**2004**	**2005**	**2006**	**2007**	**2008**	**2009**	**2010**	**2011**	**2012**	**2013**	**2014**	**2015 Req.**	**Total: FY2001-F2015**
Joint Improvised Explosive Device Defeat Fund (JIEDDF)	0	0	0	0	0	1.958	4.400	4.197	3.117	1.762	2.791	2.385	1.449	0.879	0.379	23.317
Strategic Reserve Readiness Fund acc't	0	0	0	0	0	0	1.615	0	0	0	0	0	0	0	0	1.615
Reconstruction																**10.348**
Commander's. Emergency Response Program (CERP) cap	0	0	0	0.180	0.854	0.923	0.956	1.727	1.200	1.200	0.500	0.400	0.200	0.030	0.015	8.185
Task Force for Business and Stability Operations*	0	0	0	0	0	0	0	0	0	0	0	0	0.179	0.121	0	0.300
Afghanistan Infrastructure Fund (AIF)	0	0	0	0	0	0	0	0	0	0	0.400	0.400	0.325	0.199	0	1.324
Natural Resources Risk Remediation Fd*	0	0	0.489	0	0	0	0.050	0	0	0	0	0	0	0	0	0.539

In Billions of Dollars of Budget Authority															
Accounts/ Caps	**2001**	**2002**	**2003**	**2004**	**2005**	**2006**	**2007**	**2008**	**2009**	**2010**	**2011**	**2012**	**2013**	**2014**	**2015 Req.**	**Total: FY2001-F2015**
Transfer Cap and Other	**73.500**															
War Transfer Cap*	ns	ns	2.000	3.00	4.500	4.500	6.500	6.500	6.500	4.500	4.000	4.000	3.500	4.000	4.000	57.500
Overseas Contingency Ops Transfer Fund (OCOTF)*	0	0	0	0	0	0	0	0	0	4.643	0	0	0.582	0.0	0.0	5.225
National Guard and Reserve Equipment	0	0	0	0	0	1.000	0.000	1.743	0.950	0.950	0.850	1.000	1.500	1.000	0.000	8.993
Office of Security Cooperation-Iraq cap	0	0	0	0	0	0	0	0	0	0	0	0	0.508	0.209	0.140	0.857
Europ. Reassurance Initiative Fund (ERI)	0	0	0	0	0	0	0	0	0	0	0	0	0	0	0.925	0.925
Flexible DOD	**22.934**	**15.296**	**19.56**	**6.318**	**17.359**	**18.890**	**27.975**	**41.683**	**26.221**	**32.702**	**27.485**	**22.282**	**15.05**	**12.429**	**15.333**	**321.525**
War			**7**										**3**			
Total DOD War	22.934	16.870	72.536	90.776	75.642	115.763	166.272	186.908	145.689	162.390	158.788	115.083	81.973	85.191	58.574	1,555.389
Flexible Share	**100.0%**	**90.7%**	**27.0%**	**7.0%**	**22.9%**	**16.3%**	**16.8%**	**22.3%**	**18.0%**	**20.1%**	**17.3%**	**19.4%**	**18.4%**	**14.6%**	**26.2%**	**20.7%**

Table 9. (Continued)

	In Billions of Dollars of Budget Authority															
Accounts/ Caps	**2001**	**2002**	**2003**	**2004**	**2005**	**2006**	**2007**	**2008**	**2009**	**2010**	**2011**	**2012**	**2013**	**2014**	**2015 Req.**	**Total: FY2001-F2015**
OCO Train & Equip	0	0	1.400	1.150	1.220	0.960	1.125	1.563	2.029	2.015	2.855	2.197	2.187	1.763	6.265	26.728
Base Budget Train & Equip	0	0	0	0	0.025	0.325	0.425	0.425	0.525	0.540	0.395	0.650	0.800	0.663	0.543	5.316
Total Train and Equip	**0**	**0**	**1.400**	**1.150**	**1.270**	**1.285**	**1.550**	**1.988**	**2.254**	**2.555**	**3.250**	**2.847**	**2.986**	**2.426**	**6.808**	**32.044**

Sources: National Defense Authorization Acts and DOD appropriations acts for relevant years. Defense Institute of *Security Assistance Management, Security Cooperation Programs Through Fiscal Year 2014, Revision 14.8*; http://www.disam.dsca.mil/documents/pubs/security_cooperation_programs_20140806.

Notes: * indicates transfer fund where monies are moved into other accounts during execution. Shares calculated reflect only those authorities funded in the war budget and designated as either emergency or OCO. Bracketed indicate base budget funds that are not included in the totals for war funding. Funding levels are appropriations not authorizations.

Flexibility at the Beginning of Hostilities

Congress has been willing to provide the greatest flexibility about where, how, and for what funds can be spent at the beginning of hostilities. Shortly after the 9/11 attacks, Congress appropriated $40 billion to the Emergency Response Fund (ERF) for the entire government. Of this total, $10 billion was available immediately, another $10 billion within 15 days after the Administration submitted a planned allocation, and the remaining $20 billion as specified in a subsequent appropriations act.[118]

DOD's funds to conduct operations in Afghanistan and respond to the attacks on the Pentagon and New York City were transferred to the Defense Emergency Response Fund (DERF), a newly established account. Initially, the Administration reported allocations of defense funds according to a new set of categories for wartime needs, such as "Increased Situational Awareness" (intelligence) and "Increased Worldwide posture" (operations) rather than traditional appropriations accounts.[119] These new categories were largely replaced by traditional appropriation accounts in the FY2002 Supplemental that allocated the last $20 billion.[120]

At the beginning of the Iraq invasion, the Administration requested that $75 billion be appropriated to the DERF to provide the maximum flexibility. Although Congress provided $15.6 billion in the newly- established Iraq Freedom Fund (IFF) flexible account, $59.3 billion, or most of the request, was provided in traditional appropriation accounts. DOD was given flexibility in the new IFF account to distribute funds after enactment and then report to Congress.[121]

As the Afghan and Iraq wars continued, Congress insisted that DOD receive war funding primarily in traditional accounts. For example, in FY2004 when the Administration requested $25 billion in "contingent emergency funds" to be allocated in a later request, Congress appropriated the funds to specific accounts.[122]

Congress and the FY2015 Counterterrorism Partnership Fund (CTPF)

The Administration is arguing that the same broad flexibility requested in the CTPF is necessary to respond quickly to unanticipated crises in any part of the world.[123] The rationale for the CTPF is:

- to provide counterterrorism (CT) support to partner nations by increasing "the ability of partner forces in these countries to conduct CT operations within their own borders, prevent the spillover of terrorist presence and activities from neighboring states, and participate in multinational CT operations to degrade terrorist threats" ($2.5 billion in illustrative funding);
- to address the conflict in Syria and the impact on its neighbors through a Regional Stabilization Initiative, including training and equipping the moderate Syrian opposition ($1.0 billion in illustrative funding);
- to send advisors to support Iraqi security forces to combat the Islamic State;
- to increase U.S. capabilities for Intelligence, Surveillance and Reconnaissance (ISR), helicopter, and communications and logistical capabilities (amount unspecified); and
- to establish a crisis response fund for contingencies ranging from noncombatant evacuation operations to smaller-scale combat missions ($500 million).[124]

In July 2014 congressional hearings by the House Budget Committee and the House Armed Services Committee, Members raised concerns that the funds could be "slush funds" with little control over their use, that the proposal "lack[ed] detail and is too broad in scope," would not be subject to other provisions of law, allowed the funds to be spent in any country, lacked restrictions on how the funds could be spent, and included limited congressional oversight. Some Members asked why the Administration did not simply ask to expand currently available authorities to provide logistical support to nations participating in complementary counterterrorism efforts.[125]

DOD witnesses, Deputy Secretary Robert Work and Vice-Chairman, Joint Chiefs of Staff, Admiral James Winnefeld defended the proposals, stating they were intended to "increase flexibility" beyond that already available in order to respond to an unanticipated "fast-moving situation ... or unexpected problems," that proposed spending would be subject to rigorous interagency review, and that Congress could participate because of 15-day advance notifications in line with other flexible funds.[126]

In the FY2015 Continuing Resolution (CR; H.J.Res. 124/P.L. 113-64) appropriating funds until December 11, 2014, Congress provided limited authority for the Syria Train-and-Equip part of the CTPF request. It would allow DOD to train vetted insurgent groups fighting the Islamic State under certain conditions:

- DOD would have to reprogram monies from existing DOD funds (either base or OCO), which under DOD regulations, must be approved in writing by the four congressional defense committees (authorization and appropriations); and
- the authority would sunset with the CR rather than by December 31, 2018, as requested.[127]

Much of the debate has focused on the Train-and-Equip provision for Syria, where a U.S. train-and-equip program could be complicated by the complex dynamics among non-governmental Syrian groups with varying political goals.[128] CTPF funds could also be used for any counterterrorism partner, including Somalia, Cameroon, Chad, Liberia, and Nigeria to Yemen or other countries not listed in budget justification materials.[129] While the four congressional defense committees could participate in allocation decisions under the CR because of DOD's regulatory requirement that transfers be approved by those committees, other Members would not have a voice.

The $500 million request for a Crisis Response Fund for "small combat operations" would allow the Administration to begin military operations without the need to seek appropriations.[130] This could raise concerns about whether a potentially new conflict was authorized by current Authorizations of the Use of Force or was justified by the Administration as conducted under the President's power as Commander-in- Chief.[131]

On November 10, 2014, the Administration requested $5.0 billion for DOD in an FY2015 supplemental to combat the Islamic State, including additional authority to Train and Equip Iraqi forces (see "The New Request to Counter the Islamic State").

NDAA Draft FY2015 Conference Version

The CR anticipated that Congress may revise this Train-and-Equip authority in the National Defense Authorization Act (H.R. 4435, S. 2430).[132] The draft conference version of the FY2015 NDAA (H.R. 3797), passed by the House by a vote of 300-119 on December 4, 2014, extended the language in the CR, continuing to rely on reprogramming to fund Syria Train-and-Equip activities. H.R. 3797 also reduced the DOD CTPF request from $4.0 billion to $1.3 billion for a two-year program to build partnership capacity in the Middle East and Africa (except for Iraq, separately funded) but required DOD to rely on existing authorities. The conference bill also added congressional oversight and reporting requirements.[133]

Precedents for CTPF Are More Specific

While the Administration cites precedents for the CTPF, the proposed statutory language is broader than other flexible funds approved by Congress.[134] In its scope, the CTPF request most resembles the two funds set up at the beginning of the Afghan and Iraq war, the DERF and the IFF. In terms of its purpose— building partnerships to counter terrorism—the following flexible funds created after the 9/11 attacks appear to be closer precedents. Some of these flexible funds are financed in the base budget and others with emergency/OCO-designated funds, but all are more specifically defined with lower spending levels than the CTPF (see **Table 9**).

- Set up in FY2003, "*coalition support*" allows DOD to reimburse other nations (primarily Pakistan's border operations) for logistical and military support for U.S. counterterror operations; the total amount has generally been capped at about $1.5 billion a year with funds drawn from the Operation and Maintenance, Defense-wide account (emergency/OCO-designated).[135]
- Funds were appropriated in FY2009 and FY2011 to the Pakistan Counter-Insurgency Fund to enable DOD, with State Department concurrence, to provide *counter-insurgency funds to Pakistan*; this type of funding was later transferred to the State Department/USAID (emergency/OCO-designated).[136]
- *Section 1203 authority*, authorized in the FY2013 NDAA, permits DOD to use up to $150 million in O&M monies to enhance counterterror capabilities of Yemen (up to $75 million) and Djibouti and Somalia ($150 million) (base-budget funded);
- *Section 1206 authority*, first authorized in FY2006, is designed to build the capacity of foreign military forces by training, equipping, and providing supplies to conduct counterterror operations jointly with the United States or on their own; DOD could tap funds within Operation and Maintenance (O&M) accounts up to a statutory cap generally set at $200 million to $300 million annually (base budget-funded).

- *Another Section 1206 authority*, "Support foreign forces disarming the Lord's Resistance Army (LRA)," permits DOD to provide support to Ugandan-led military operations to capture or kill LRA commanders, and is set at $50 million annually (base-budget funded).[137]
- *Section 1207*, Security and Stabilization Assistance, authorized from FY2006 to FY2010, permits DOD to provide security assistance for stability operations at the request of the Secretary of State within a spending cap set annually at about $100 million.[138]
- A new *Global Security Contingency Fund* was authorized in FY2012 to allow DOD to transfer up to $350 million from other accounts to enhance the capabilities of other countries' military forces to conduct border security, internal defense, counterterrorism, and support U.S. stability operations (base-budget funded).[139]
- Authority for "*global lift and sustain*" (10 U.S.C. Sec. 27d) and specific Iraq and Afghanistan lift and sustain authorizations in NDAAs allow DOD to provide logistical support to foreign nations participating in counterterror operations with the United States ($400 million funding for Afghanistan) (Emergency/OCO funded).[140]

In each of these cases, Congress restricted the Administration's requests for broadly-defined authorities, (i.e., eliminated statutory clauses "notwithstanding other provisions of law" that exempted the authority from all other laws), reduced spending limits, and added reporting requirements. Generally, authorized funding levels were set for one, two, or several years, requiring Congress to revisit the program's parameters; in a few cases, the amount was set for each fiscal year.[141]

Some of these Train-and-Equip authorities were funded within other accounts up to statutory caps, and could require some trade-offs with other programs if the amount was not anticipated in DOD's budgeting. Setting caps provides less flexibility than providing specifically dedicated funding in a separate appropriation account.

With the exception of support for Pakistan's counterterror operations on the border with Afghanistan to reimburse logistical support, funding levels for other partnership-building activities are below the CTPF request, ranging from a low of $25 million a year for Sec. 1207 activities for irregular forces working with U.S. special operations teams to $350 million for Sec. 1206 Global Train-and-Equip activities to train and aid counterterrorism efforts of other countries (**Table 9**).

The Administration's FY2015 DOD request of $4 billion is roughly five times as much as the sum of other Train-and-Equip authorities, excluding funds that reimburse Pakistan border operations.[142] Funds in the CTPF would also be additional appropriations rather than drawn from other accounts and would be available for three years rather than one year. An additional $1.0 billion is also requested for the State Department to use for its own set of tools for broadly defined goals.[143]

Do Train-and-Equip Programs Work: The Effectiveness Issue

In deciding whether to approve the Administration's proposal to "scale up" Train-and-Equip programs for counterterrorism partners, a key question is whether earlier similar programs have been effective. Despite extensive studies, there does not appear to be any consensus that such programs are generally successful. Rather, a wide variety of problems have been identified, ranging from the "patchwork" of current legal authorities to the complexities of U.S. intervention in another country's military whose goals, operating practices, and political constraints may be very different.

In a 2013 study, the RAND Corporation found that there were 165 security cooperation programs, requiring DOD professionals to pull together a "patchwork" of ways to build partner capacity and provide security assistance. Together, the RAND study suggested, this patchwork "is more a tangled web, with holes, overlaps, and confusions," where several funding sources and programs may support individual events or initiatives by DOD and the State Department.[144] This study argues that the lack of multi-year, flexible authorities, limitations and regional focus of particular authorities, and coordination and congressional reporting requirements "hinder[s] effective planning and efficient execution." It also recommends expanding authority to build partnership authority and counterterrorism training.[145]

At the same time, the study acknowledges that evaluating the effectiveness of current programs is difficult because of data limitations, lack of assessments, and the long time horizon for partnership efforts. The study also observes that showing the relationship between upgrading indigenous forces and reducing the need for U.S. combat forces to intervene—the underlying rationale for the CTPF—"is not a straightforward endeavor."[146]

Another problem identified in two other RAND studies is that most assessments "if they are done at all, are largely conducted by the same organizations that executed the activities," and "are subject to concerns about bias," or by program managers who lack the longevity needed to evaluate these programs. While officials claim that relationships improve with partnership programs, that does not necessarily mean that Train-and-Equip programs were effective in improving military capabilities.[147]

In response to criticism, DOD conducted assessments of several Sec. 1206 programs. While DOD found a general improvement in the ability of recipients to conduct counterterrorism or stability operations using the equipment provided, there were limitations in "absorptive capacity" and the sustainability of programs (particularly for training and logistics) as Sec. 1206 funding was withdrawn.[148]

An ambitious statistical evaluation of 29 partner nations since World War II by RAND found several factors key to success:

- on the partner's side: shared security goals, financial participation, high governance, and strong economy;
- on the U.S. side: consistency in funding and implementation, matching the absorptive capacity of the partner, and including sustainment mechanisms.

The study did not, however, identify whether these conditions were generally the case.[149] In more recent cases, Train-and-Equip programs are more likely to be initiated in failing or unstable states.

A recent 2014 RAND study reiterates the importance of the factors cited in its 2013 study, but emphasizes the difficulties in ensuring that the goals of the United States and partner nations are compatible, particularly when the United States is working with insurgency groups or non-state actors whose control of forces and support from the general population may be problematic, factors relevant to Syria. Other complications are the difficulty in getting consistent, long-term support from both the legislative and executive branches of government, and unanticipated consequences of U.S. intervention. At the same time, the study concludes that doing nothing could also be harmful.[150]

In January 2014, President Obama acknowledged the uncertainties in the effectiveness of Train-and- Equip programs for insurgency groups, noting that when the CIA looked for examples of cases when U.S. financing and supplying of arms to an insurgency worked out well, "they couldn't come up with much."[151] Overt Train-and-Equip operations could be equally if not more problematic.

Training Afghan and Iraqi Security Forces

In some ways, U.S. efforts over the past decade to train and support operations, and pay and equip armed and police forces of the Afghanistan Security Forces Fund (ASFF) and Iraq Security Forces Funds (ISFF), are much larger versions of Train-and-Equip programs. While other Train-and-Equip programs are intended to substitute for U.S. forces before intervention, ASFF and ISFF funding is intended to create capable, independent forces to enable the United States forces to leave.[152]

U.S. funding requests generally reflect plans to develop security forces by a certain date.[153] Initially funded at $150 million, annual support of the ASFF peaked at $11.6 billion in FY2010. Since then, funding has declined to $4 billion-$5 billion a year, a level DOD predicts is likely to continue to be needed for several years in light of the limited resources of the Afghan government (**Table 10**).

Funding for the ISFF fluctuated between $3.0 billion and $5.7 billion between FY2004 and FY2008. In 2008, Congress became reluctant to pay for Iraqi security forces as Iraqi government revenues rose with the upswing in oil prices.[154] After that, funding fell to about $1 billion annually to zero in FY2012, as Iraqis took over funding and operational responsibility and U.S. troops withdrew (**Table 10**).

In addition to requiring Iraq to share the burden of rebuilding Iraqi security forces in the FY2008 Supplemental (P.L. 110-252), Congress adopted other restrictions in funding "infrastructure" projects, including those to rebuild security forces in the FY2008 Supplemental, and required reports on the readiness and transfer of responsibility to Iraqi units, as well as the overall cost to train both Iraqi and Afghan security forces.[155] The Administration did not provide estimates of total costs for either Iraq or Afghanistan.[156]

Over the years, Congress and others have voiced many concerns about these training programs, including the performance of contractors; coordination between DOD, State Department, and NATO coalition efforts; shortages in trainers; government corruption; absenteeism; illiteracy; and high levels of attrition of local forces. Other concerns center on the capabilities of indigenous forces to conduct operations, and maintain and sustain security forces. As the United States withdraws forces in Afghanistan, the Special Inspector General for Afghanistan (SIGAR) raised the issue of how to conduct oversight. Despite such concerns, Congress has generally provided DOD with most, if not all, of the funds requested because the withdrawal of U.S. troops depends on the success of these efforts.[157]

Table 10. Funding for the ASFF and the ISFF, FY2004-FY2015 Request

Account	In Billions of Dollars													
	Fiscal Year													
	04	05	06	07	08	09	10	11	12	13	14	15	04-14	04-15 Req.
Afghan. Security Forces Fund[a]	0.3	1.3	1.9	7.4	2.8	5.6	9.2	11.6	10.2	5.1	4.7	4.1	60.1	64.3
Iraq Security Forces Fund[a]	5.0	5.7	3.0	5.5	3.0	1.0	1.0	1.5	0.0	0.0	0.0	0.0	25.7	25.7
Total	5.3	7.0	4.9	12.9	5.8	6.6	10.2	13.1	10.2	5.1	4.7	4.1	85.9	90.0

Sources: Public laws, congressional appropriations reports, DOD budget justification materials, and DOD Cost of War Update Reports; FY2013 is post-sequestration level. Reflects budget authority as originally appropriated, excluding later rescissions.

Notes:

a. Appropriated to the State Department appropriations in FY2004 but transferred to DOD for implementation.

Assessing Iraq Security Forces

Beginning in 2005, Congress required a report entitled "Measuring Stability and Security in Iraq" that assessed the training and development of the Iraqi security forces, including both the armed services, the police, and other paramilitary forces that together reportedly total 666,500.158 In late November 2014, Iraqi Prime Minister Haider al-Abadi reported that Iraqi security forces paid salaries to 50,000 "ghost" soldiers not in military service.[159]

In its June 2010 report, the last report issued as U.S. troops were transitioning to advising and assisting Iraqi forces, the security environment was characterized as stable but "fragile," with declining levels of violence despite activities by some Sunni insurgents, Al Qaeda in Iraq, and Shia extremist groups. The report complimented the Iraqi security forces on providing security during the March 7, 2010, elections. Despite some logistics and sustainment issues, DOD predicted that the Iraqi security forces would reach Minimum Essential Capability (MEC), the level needed for internal security, when U.S. forces left.[160]

Overall, the report concluded:

> In spite of progress this period, challenges remain. Violent extremist networks, while significantly degraded, are still able to execute attacks. Tensions will remain high until the government is seated. Iraq remains fragile, primarily because many underlying sources of political instability have yet to be resolved.[161]

In a November 2011 hearing, when it was clear that all U.S. forces would withdraw from Iraq by the end of December 2011 because a Bilateral Security Agreement with the Iraqi government that would exempt U.S. forces from Iraqi law could not be reached, then-Secretary of Defense Leon Panetta remained confident of the abilities of Iraqi security forces stating that

> While these groups remain capable of conducting these types [high-profile] of attacks, they do not enjoy widespread support among the Iraqi population, and more importantly, the Iraqis have developed some of the most capable counterterrorism forces in the region.[162]

Iraqi officials and Iraqi public opinion (particularly Sunnis) were not optimistic about the Iraqi Security Forces' capabilities and legitimacies, as reported in an extensive after-action RAND report commissioned by DOD.[163]

After U.S. troops left, the United States continued its security relationship through arms sales administered by the Office of Security Cooperation–Iraq and the State Department, which took over police training.[164] In the spring of 2013, the Chief of the Office of Security Cooperation, General Robert Caslen, voiced confidence about the capabilities of the Iraqi Navy, Air Force, and Counter-Terrorism Service, though with some concerns about Iraqi Army units stationed in cities where they competed with provincial governments and the Iraqi police.[165]

Some observers suggest that the weaknesses in the Iraqi security forces did not become apparent until 2013 because they did not face significant challenges from insurgencies. A December 2013 study by the Center for Strategic and International Affairs noted deterioration in Iraqi military capabilities, a push by President Maliki to install loyalists and marginalize Sunnis, and considerable corruption in both the armed forces and the police.[166]

After a November 2013 visit where Prime Minister Maliki requested more U.S. military help to counter rising threats from internal insurgencies and spillover from the Syrian civil war, Senators John McCain, Carl Levin, James Inhofe, Robert Menendez, Bob Corker, and Lindsey Graham wrote to President Obama that "Prime Minister Maliki's mismanagement of Iraqi politics is contributing to the recent surge in violence," and that additional

U.S. arms sales should be part of a comprehensive Iraqi strategy that addresses the political sources of current violence.[167]

Although the United States increased arms sales, the weaknesses in the Iraqi military became apparent between December 2013 and February 2014 when Iraqi Security Forces proved unable to recapture Fallujah and Ramadi from Islamic State forces.[168] By May 2014 the Iraqi Army had still not recaptured Fallujah and barely held onto to Ramadi despite dispatching 42,000 troops, and was plagued by mass desertions and an inability to gain the loyalty of Sunni tribesman in Anbar province.[169] The collapse of Iraqi security forces was not anticipated and may reflect an underestimate by the United States of the effects of endemic corruption, President Maliki's sectarianism, and the limitations of the Train-and-Equip program in ensuring that Iraqi security forces could provide adequate logistical support or sustain operations in the face of insurgent attacks.

Assessing Afghan Security Forces

Congress also required a detailed assessment of the Afghan security forces in the semi-annual Section 1230 report on Progress Toward Security and Stability in Afghanistan in the FY2008 National Defense Authorization Act (P.L. 110-181). While the latest report describes progress by the Afghans in taking over security responsibilities from U.S. troops, it also acknowledges serious longstanding problems from corruption and personnel attrition.[170]

Similar to the Iraq experience, corruption in Afghan security forces remains a serious concern, including both contractual corruption and the buying and selling of officer billets. At the same time, sectarian divisions are seen as less of a problem with Afghan army and police units generally being balanced ethnically.[171] In terms of capabilities, the Afghan security forces show some of the same weaknesses as Iraqi security forces—in logistics, sustainment, officer quality, and contract administration.[172] In addition, Afghan security forces face persistent problems in attrition, where about 30% of personnel need to be replaced each year.[173]

Although Afghan security forces continue to be tested by Taliban insurgent attacks, some observers remain concerned that the U.S. troop withdrawal may occur at a time when Afghan security forces may not be able to sustain its forces without U.S. support. An extensive evaluation required by the FY2013 National Defense Authorization Act raised familiar concerns about weaknesses in Afghan logistical, contracting, intelligence, and communication capabilities, and concluded that Afghan security forces would not be able to effectively meet an enhanced Taliban threat in the next few years if the planned reduction in U.S. and allied assistance occurred.[174]

The Special Inspector General for Afghanistan (SIGAR) also reported buildup in unobligated balances, signaling slower-than-anticipated execution of plans, as well as changes in the size of Afghan security forces, prompting some reductions by Congress. The SIGAR has also voiced concerns about the difficulty in maintaining oversight of U.S. funding for ASFF and other reconstruction funding as the U.S. presence shrinks.[175]

Meeting Unanticipated Wartime Needs Quickly

In the past 13 years, Congress has set up and provided appropriations in a lump sum to special accounts to meet unanticipated wartime needs as quickly as possible.

- The largest annual appropriation was the $16.8 billion provided by Congress in FY2008 to a newly established Mine Resistant Ambush Program (MRAP) account to purchase, train, and transport MRAPS vehicles that provide better protection than armored Humvees against Improvised Explosive Devices (IED), the signature threat of both the Afghan and Iraq wars;
- The Joint Improvised Explosive Device Defeat Fund (JIEDDF), set up in FY2006 with a $2.0 billion appropriation, was to provide funds to develop, buy, and field devices to counter Improvised Explosive Devices (IEDs) which permitted funds to be shifted to procurement, RDT&E, or operation and maintenance accounts as needed.
- The Joint Urgent Operational Needs account was a successor to the Rapid Acquisition Fund, both set up to provide a lump sum that could be allocated quickly to meet unanticipated war needs, bypassing normal appropriation accounts.

Wartime Reconstruction Accounts

Congress created two other wartime programs intended to improve relationships between U.S. troops and the local population by funding local reconstruction needs. The first, the Commander's Emergency Response Program (CERP), was established in 2003, to provide funds to local commanders to "respond to urgent humanitarian relief and reconstruction requirements within their area of responsibilities ... that will immediately assist the Iraqi people ... and fund a similar program to assist the people of Afghanistan."[176] Funding for this program peaked at $1.2 billion in FY2007 and has fallen steadily as U.S. troops have been withdrawn from Iraq and Afghanistan (**Table 9**).

Over the years, as concerns rose about the size and effectiveness of CERP projects, Congress expanded reporting requirements, and set up the Afghan Infrastructure Fund (AIF) in FY2011 to fund larger projects. The Special Inspector Generals for Iraq and for Afghanistan criticized CERP for its selection of projects, corruption, management problems, and effectiveness. The IGs also raised concerns about whether the Afghan or Iraqi government would continue to fund larger reconstruction projects after U.S. support ended. The Task Force for Business and Stability Operations was established as a separate account in FY2011 to stimulate private sector growth by encouraging foreign investment in Afghanistan.[177]

Traditional Transfer Authority

For the past decade, Congress has set annual caps on transfers between DOD accounts for both non-war funds and emergency or OCO-designated funds. DOD can transfer funds from one account to another if the activity is for a higher priority and based on unforeseen military requirements, after receiving written approval from the four congressional defense committees. DOD can also reprogram funds within an account from one activity to another, as long as the purpose remains the same.[178]

For the base budget, transfer caps are generally between $3 billion and $4 billion, or less than 1% of total DOD base budget funding. Recognizing the greater uncertainty in predicting wartime spending, DOD appropriations acts have typically set a cap for war funds of about $4 billion, or about 3.5% of total war funds in a year, over three times the cap set for base budget funds.[179]

The New Request to Counter the Islamic State

On November 10, 2014, the Administration submitted a FY2015 budget amendment of $5.5 billion in OCO funds—$5 billion for DOD and $520 million for the Department of State—to support efforts to combat the Islamic

State (IS) after its takeover of territory in Iraq and Syria. The November amendment would increase DOD's OCO request from $58.6 billion to $63.6 billion (**Table 13**).

Several budgetary and policy questions may be raised about the new $5.0 billion budget amendment funding military action against the Islamic State:

- Could all or some of the additional $5.0 billion request be accommodated within the original $58.6 billion request since there are indications that DOD's June request may be larger than needed?[180]
- What are the pros and cons of the new Train-and-Equip authority for Iraq, and how might it be modified to narrow its scope and increase congressional oversight? Is the cost- sharing arrangement proposed practical?
- Would Congress want to include restrictions on the missions of U.S. troops deployed in Iraq or in Syria?

Department of Defense Request

As of November 20, 2014, DOD estimated that $855 million had been spent to conduct the IS campaign, an average of $8.1 million a day.[181] Initially, DOD financed airstrikes and the deployment of U.S. military personnel to Iraq to conduct an assessment and provide advice using OCO funds already appropriated for FY2014. Starting October 1, 2014, DOD tapped OCO-designated funds in the FY2015 CR. For example, DOD used OCO-designated FY2015 Navy O&M and Air Force O&M funds to conduct air strikes in Iraq and Syria, based on the type of expenses involved. This practice of relying on current funding until supplemental funding is provided later in the year is known as "cash flowing."

Starting October 1, 2014, incremental costs of the new Iraq and Syria operations (named Operation Inherent Resolve) are being paid for from funds appropriated by Congress in the FY2015 Continuing Resolution (CR, H.J.Res. 124/P.L. 113-164). Under the CR, OCO for DOD is appropriated at a rate of operations based on the $85.4 billion in OCO funds enacted in FY2014. This is $26.6 billion above the FY2015 request of $58.6 billion.

On November 10, 2014, DOD submitted an amendment to its FY2015 OCO request for an additional $5.0 billion (Table 11).

Table 11. DOD's OCO Funding: FY2014 Enacted to FY2015 Supplemental Request

In Billions of Dollars of Budget Authority					
Title	**FY2014 Enacted (P.L. 113-76)**	**FY2015 Request[a]**	**FY2015 CR (H.J.Res. 24)[b]**	**FY2015 Amendment[c]**	**Total FY2015 Req.**
Military Personnel	8.15	5.45	8.15	0.14	5.60
Operation and Maintenance	69.68	42.07	69.68	2.32	44.38
Procurement	7.11	6.03	7.11	0.83	6.86
RDT&E	0.14	0.08	0.14	0.14	0.22
Military Construction	0.00	0.05	0.00	0.00	0.05
Family Housing	0.00	0.00	0.00	0.00	0.00
Revolving and Mgt. Funds	0.26	0.09	0.26	0.00	0.09
Iraq Train and Equip	0.00	0.00	0.00	1.62	1.62
Counterterrorism Partnerships Fund (CTPF)	0.00	4.00	0.00	0.00	4.00
European Reassurance Initiative (ERI)	0.00	0.93	0.00	0.00	0.93
Total OCO	85.34	58.69	85.34	5.05	63.74
Rescissions	na	-0.12	na	0.00	-0.12
Total OCO Adjusted	**85.35**	**58.57**	**85.35**	**5.05**	**63.62**

Source: Table 1 in Department of Defense, Fiscal Year 2015 Budget Amendment, Overview, Overseas Contingency Operations, June 2014, http://comptroller.defense.gov/Portals/45/Documents/defbudget/fy2015/amendment/FY2015_Budget_Request_Overview_Book_Amended.pdf, and DOD, Office of the Under Secretary of Defense (Comptroller) Fiscal Year (FY) 2015 Overseas Contingency Operations (OCO) Budget Amendment Update, November 2014, http://comptroller.defense.gov/Portals/45/Documents/defbudget/fy2015/amendment/FY15_OCO_Budget_Amendment_Update.pdf.

Notes:

a. Reflects DOD amended OCO request for Afghan war and Office of Security Cooperation-Iraq, submitted June 2014.

b. Estimates of annualized budget authority. The FY2015 CR provides OCO budget authority at a rate for operations through December 11, 2014.

c. Reflects DOD's FY2015 amended OCO request of November 10, 2014, to conduct Operation Inherent Resolve (OIR) against the Islamic State of Iraq and the Levant in Syria and Iraq. Except for the FY2015 amendment, there are no funds to counter IS.

The November 10, 2014, amended DOD/OCO FY2015 request of $5.0 billion is for:

- incremental military personnel expenses (e.g., hardship pay) for U.S. military supporting Operation Inherent Resolve (OIR);
- fuel, supplies, and repair costs for ground operations, flying hours, and steaming hours of ships in the region, as well as other support;
- command, control, and intelligence activities, and intelligence, surveillance, and reconnaissance (ISR), and classified activities;
- replacement of expended munitions (e.g., Hellfire, Maverick, Tomahawks); and
- building the capacity of Iraqi security forces and Kurdish and tribal forces, providing support to coalition members, and other small-scale humanitarian relief and reconstruction.[182]

New Iraq Train-and-Equip Authority

Under its request for broad authority to train and equip Iraqi and other security forces, DOD would

> provide assistance to military and other security forces of, or associated with, the Government of Iraq, including Kurdish and tribal security forces, with a national security mission, to counter the Islamic State in Iraq and the Levant, including the provision o0f equipment, supplies, services, training, facility and infrastructure repair, renovation, construction, and stipends.... [183]

The Administration is also requesting authority for the Secretary of Defense to waive "any other provision of law that would otherwise prohibit, restrict, limit or otherwise constrain the obligation or expenditure of [these] funds."[184] Typically, Congress has not accepted this kind of exception.

In order to be fully obligated, the proposal would require Iraqi, Kurdish, and tribal security forces to contribute 40% of the $1.6 billion DOD request (including in-kind contributions), with at least half of that contribution to come from the government of Iraq. Arms sales could not count toward the contribution.[185] DOD obligations would be capped at 60% of the total or $972 million until the 40% ($647 million) contribution—in cash or in-kind—from Iraq and Kurdish and tribal security forces is received. The draft conference agreement of the FY2015 NDAA deletes the exclusion of arms sales, which would presumably permit arms sales to count as part of the contribution. The Secretary of Defense would monitor the contribution level.[186]

The Administration is also asking to expand current coalition support authorities to include reimbursing Iraq for logistical support of U.S. forces. In addition, $15 million more would be provided for "emergencies and extraordinary payments" for "confidential military purposes," typically intelligence support.[187]

Like the Syria Train-and-Equip authority already proposed, the new Iraqi Train-and-Equip authority would be used with not only the Iraq army and police force, but also Kurdish and tribal groups. It could encounter some of the same difficulties and politico-military complications of the proposed Syria Train- and-Equip authority temporarily authorized in the FY2015 CR. Another potential issue is the likelihood of success. Previous U.S. efforts to train and equip foreign militaries—both covert by the CIA and overt— have often proved problematic (See the section "Do Train-and-Equip Programs Work: The Effectiveness Issue.")

Additional U.S. Military Personnel

DOD's additional request would increase U.S. troop strength in and around Iraq and Afghanistan by some 4,000 in FY2015, including troops providing training and assistance in Iraq as well as providing additional support in the region. If the overall FY2015 OCO request is approved, troop strength in and around Iraq and Afghanistan would total 79,047 including 64,482 providing in-theater support (**Table 12**).

Predicting Future Costs

Predicting future costs of the new U.S. role in countering the Islamic State is difficult because of the nature of the air campaign and uncertainties about whether the U.S. mission may expand. Compared to other, earlier air campaigns, counter-ISIL operations are more episodic and reactive because targets are less predictable. U.S. operations in Libya during Operation Odyssey Dawn in 2011 focused on supporting other coalition partners' air operations, with some interdiction of pro-Qadhafi units threatening civilian populations. Earlier, during Operation Allied Force in Serbia and Kosovo (1999), air operations targeted infrastructure, particularly military bases and airfields, along with electrical and broadcast centers.

Table 12. U.S. Military Strength, FY2014-FY2015, Amended OCO

	FY2014 Enacted	FY2015 CR	FY2015 Request	FY2015 Supp.	Total FY2015 Req.
Afghanistan (OEF)	37,234	ns	11,661	0	11,661
Iraq (OIR)	0	ns	0	2,904	2,904
In-theater Support	61,071	ns	63,309	1,173	64,482
Total	**98,305**	**ns**	**74,970**	**4,077**	**79,047**

Sources: Figure 2 in Department of Defense, Fiscal Year 2015 Budget Amendment, Overview, Overseas Contingency Operations, June 2014, http://comptroller.defense.gov/Portals/45/Documents/defbudget/fy2015/amendment/FY2015_Budget_Request_Overview_Book_Amended.pdf; and DOD, Office of the Under Secretary of Defense (Comptroller) Fiscal Year (FY) 2015 Overseas Contingency Operations (OCO) Budget Amendment Update, November 2014, http://comptroller.defense.gov/Portals/45/Documents/defbudget/fy2015/amendment/ FY15_OCO_Budget_Amendment_Update.pdf.

Notes: Figures reflect average strength.

a. Figure 2 in the FY2015 November request appears to include an error, showing 2,577 as the sum of 2,904 additional troops in Iraq and 1,173 providing in-theater support; this table corrects that error.

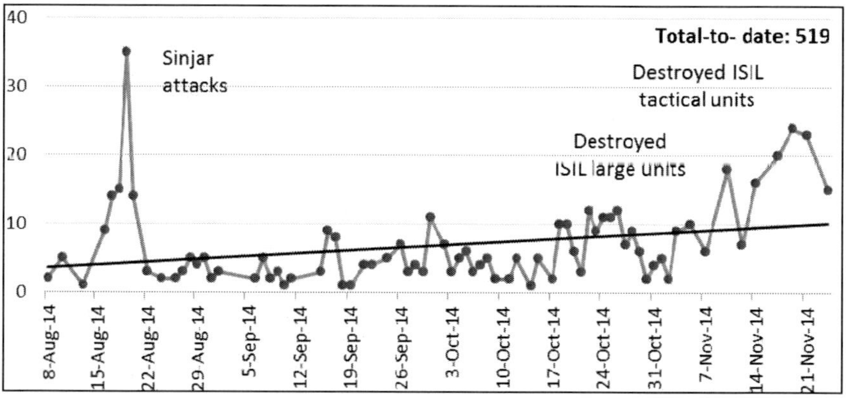

Sources: CRS compilation of data from DOD press releases; see also DOD website on Operation Inherent Resolve, http://www.defense.gov/home/features/2014/0814_iraq/.

Figure 10. U.S. Airstrikes in Iraq, August 8, 2014-November 24, 2014.

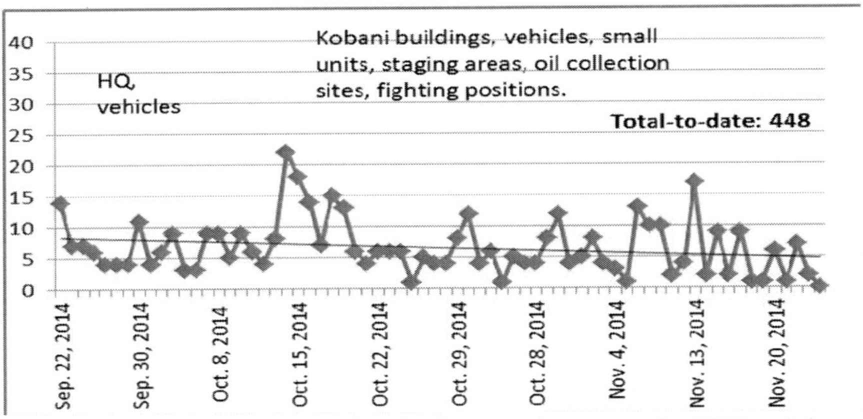

Sources: CRS compilation of data from DOD press releases; see also DOD website on Operation Inherent Resolve, http://www.defense.gov/home/features/2014/0814_iraq/.

Figure 11. U.S. Air Strikes in Syria, September 22-November 24, 2014.

By contrast, ISIL has few fixed facilities, and attacks tend to focus on "targets of opportunity," which can be units or trucks and other equipment supporting ISIL operations (**Figure 10** and **Figure 11**). Compared to an attack on a base or infrastructure, it can be difficult to determine the effect of a given attack. This kind of operation also provides a challenge to estimating costs. With a fixed target set, it is comparatively straightforward to determine the number of strikes and re-strikes required to destroy the targets and prevent their reconstitution. In the current situation, the number and type of strikes largely depend on the level of ISIL activity so that extrapolating future costs from experience may not be accurate.[188]

Future War Costs and Paying for an "Enduring Presence"

The President's Afghanistan withdrawal plan calls for:

- 9,800 U.S. troops in Afghanistan as of January 1, 2015 (the end of the first quarter of FY2015) to train and assist Afghan security forces and conduct counter-terrorism operations;

- about 4,900 U.S. troops by January 1, 2015, a halving; and
- an "embassy" presence of about 1,000 with unspecified counterterrorism forces.[189]

According to recent reports, the Administration is considering keeping more U.S. troops in Afghanistan at least into the spring of 2014 to make up for shortages in training capacity due to delays in commitments of ISAF allies to commit troops. There may also be pressure to retain troops because of the Administration's recent agreement to expand the mission of U.S. forces to include providing air support and sometimes accompanying Iraqi ground troops on operations.[190]

At the September 4, 2014, Wales summit, International Security Assistance Force (ISAF), made up of United States and its allies supporting Afghanistan, "reaffirmed their commitment" to Operation Resolute Support, the "non-combat train, advise, and assist mission in Afghanistan beyond 2014." There were no specific funding commitments beyond 2015. If the Afghan government signed a Bilateral Security Agreement (BSA), ISAF agreed to "contribute significantly to the financial sustainment of the ANSF [Afghan National Security Force] throughout the decade of transformation."[191] On September 30, 2014, the United States and Afghanistan signed the Bilateral Security Agreement, the day after President Ghani succeeded President Karzai, who had been unwilling to sign the agreement.[192]

In light of this potential, long-term commitment, and the current presence of over 60,000 U.S. troops in the region, Congress may have to face the issue of whether and how much DOD funding would be needed in later years and whether those funds should continue to be designated as OCO—and exempt from budget limits—or whether paying for a U.S. "enduring presence" mission like the U.S. military in South Korea or Japan should be carried in the base budget.

Post-withdrawal expenses that might or might not be considered "OCO" could possibly include the cost of

- residual U.S. troops in the region or the "enduring presence";
- continued support of the Afghan security forces in the next decade;
- continued or expanded funding of Train-and-Equip programs with partner countries; and

- reset and reconstitution of equipment, Army and Marine Corps excess strength from the earlier planned force structure expansion, and some Intelligence, Surveillance, and Reconnaissance (ISR) programs, as proposed in the FY2015 CTPF request.

In August, 2014, press reports suggested that DOD would soon issue "migration guidance" to the services for the FY2016 budget that would identify areas currently funded as OCO that would be folded back into the base budget.[193] More recently, DOD Deputy Secretary Robert Work suggested that OCO funding should be continued but under stricter rules.[194] Recently, DOD Comptroller Mike McCord suggested that DOD is negotiating with OMB to retain the OCO budget for the next couple of years in order to fund global counterterrorism while dealing with spending limits imposed by the BCA. Some observers cite the Islamic State (IS) threat along with Russian actions in the Ukraine as justifications for continuing OCO- designated funding.[195]

Although Congress did not consider the Administration's request for funding above BCA caps in DOD's FY2015 budget request, some Members are calling for lifting sequester caps in later years.[196] Assuming that current BCA budget caps are maintained, DOD would need to reduce its planned funding for the FY2012-FY2021 decade by $176 billion or 3.3% to meet BCA caps. Under these caps, DOD's funding would grow from $496 billion in FY2015 to $499 billion in FY2016, essentially a spending freeze that would not cover inflation. After that, DOD funding is slated to increase by about $12 billion annually under the sequester caps until FY2021, a "real" freeze that would largely cover inflation. The migration of some or all OCO-designated costs to the base budget would increase budgetary pressures.

Questions That Could Be Raised

There are several questions that Congress may wish to raise about future war costs.

- Are Afghan security forces likely to be able to ensure security as U.S. troops withdraw?

- Should the current 60,000 troops in the region providing "enduring presence" (like U.S. troops in Japan) be considered an OCO or base budget cost?
- Should RDT&E and procurement programs designed to counter Improvised Explosive Devices (IEDs), a standard tool of insurgents, be classified as OCO or base budget costs?
- Is the $5.0 billion requested for the Counterterrorism Partnership Fund (CTPF) to train, equip, and develop the capabilities of other countries to counter terrorist threats an OCO cost or a set of tools developed to meet current U.S. counterterrorism strategy?
- Is the European Reassurance Fund request of $925 million in FY2015 in response to actions by President Putin of Russia a temporary OCO expense or part of basic U.S. defense strategy?
- Does the requirement to meet BCA caps justify loosening the definition of war-related costs?

Alternate Residual War Funding Projections

Below are several projections of residual war costs that may reflect responses to these questions, as well as expectations about developments in Afghanistan.

One uncertainty is whether Afghan security forces will be capable of sustaining gains against the Taliban achieved in partnership with ISAF forces once U.S. and ISAF troops withdraw. Drawdown supporters cite the most recent DOD report that says that the Afghan National Security Forces (ANSF) have increasingly demonstrated their ability to plan and conduct independent and combined operations that employed multiple ANSF capabilities, disrupted the insurgency, protected the populace, and prevented the Taliban from disrupting recent national elections or holding "any significant terrain."[197] This report also notes a decline in enemy-initiated attacks by some 30%, with 80% of these attacks occurring in regions where 46% of the population lives.[198]

Others argue that Afghanistan may have difficulty sustaining its security once ISAF troops leave because the "overall trend is one of escalating violence and insurgent attacks" with continuing fighting, as well as because the ability of the insurgents to mount larger assaults reduces the likelihood of peace talks.[199] Other assessments conclude that the security environment will become increasingly challenging after ISAF forces leave.[200]

Table 13 shows several projections of long-term war costs, based on somewhat different scenarios or rationales:

- the Administration's $33.0 billion annual "placeholder" figure for OCO costs for FY2016-FY2021 in its FY2015 10-year budget plan;[201]
- CBO's projection of long-term war costs under "current law" growing from $87 billion in FY2015 to $98 billion in FY2021, reflecting a continuation of the enacted amount with increases for inflation;
- CBO's alternate policy projection that assumes war costs decline to $30 billion as troop levels drop from current levels to 30,000 by 2017; and [202]
- CRS's estimate that assumes war costs decrease to $20 billion by FY2017 as troops in the region decline from 60,000 to 38,000, and then fall to $15 billion a year from FY2019- FY2024.

Administration's FY2015 Plan

The Administration's original FY2015 projection shows war funding falling from $85 billion in FY2015 to a series of $30 billion annual placeholders from FY2016-FY2021. [203] There is no war funding shown for the rest of the decade. The Administration does not cite any particular scenario in terms of troop levels in Afghanistan or the region. Instead, the Administration has argued that the uncertainties are too great to estimate war spending beyond the request year. Each year, however, the placeholder figure has declined as the President has announced decreases in troop levels.

In the past several years, the Administration has also proposed a multiyear $450 billion cap on war funding over the next 10 years that has not, up to now, achieved legislative traction, and is no longer congruent with the latest 10-year total of $265 billion. The Administration's FY2015 Mid-Session July 2014 update reflects the specific $58.6 billion DOD war request submitted in June 2014 and increases the annual placeholder figure from $30 billion to $33 billion (**Table 13**).[204]

Table 13. Alternative Residual War Funding Projections: FY2016-FY2024

Projections	In Billions of Dollars of Budget Authority														
				Fiscal Year								Total			
	2011	**2012**	**2013**	**2014**	**2015**	**2016**	**2017**	**2018**	**2019**	**2020**	**2021**	**2022**	**2023**	**2024**	**15-19**	**15-24**
Administration FY2015 Plan	159	127	93	92	85	30	30	30	30	30	30	0	0	0	**205**	**265**
CBO Baseline Estimate[a]	159	127	99	86	87	89	90	92	94	96	98	0	0	0	**452**	**646**
CBO Alternative: 30K troops by 2017[b]	159	127	99	86	58	44	30	30	30	30	30	30	30	30	**191**	**340**
FY2015 OMB Mid- Session Update[c]	159	127	93	92	59	33	33	33	33	33	33	0	0	0	**199**	**265**

Sources: OMB, Table 28-1, Analytical Perspectives; CBO, Budget and Economic Outlook, August 2014 update.

Notes: The Administration and CBO's figures do not distinguish between DOD and war costs of State/USAID.

CBO's Baseline Estimate

CBO is required to provide a baseline estimate each year, which reflects either the latest enacted level increased to cover inflation or statutory requirements.[205] There are no statutory controls on future war funding, so CBO's projection extrapolates from the latest enacted level, in this case the $86 billion appropriated in FY2014 with increases to cover inflation. Under this scenario, war costs rise from $87 billion in FY2015 to $98 billion in FY2021 and total $646 billion over the next ten years (**Table 13**).

In the past several years, both the Administration and some Members have proposed using "savings" from this baseline projection (or current services level) of war funding to "pay for" other legislative changes. Typically, savings are calculated by subtracting a proposed statutory cap over 10 years from CBO's baseline projection, with the difference or "savings" allocated to other purposes from deficit reduction to expanded benefits for veterans.[206]

These proposals are criticized by some analysts as "budget gimmickry." CBO has pointed out that since war spending is appropriated in annual discretionary spending, a multi-year cap would not be binding. Moreover, war spending reflects policy decisions about planned troop levels rather than continuing indefinitely at the same level.[207]

CBO's Alternative Policy Projection

Because of these considerations, CBO has also produced alternative policy projections of war spending that reflect specific assumptions about future troop levels. In FY2015, for example, CBO's alternative war funding projection assumes that troops will decline from about 100,000 U.S. troops deployed in country and in the region in 2014 to 70,000 in 2015, 50,000 in 2016, and 30,000 in 2017, remaining at that level through FY2024. These CBO estimates do not reflect troop levels in particular countries and include proportionate reductions in diplomatic operations and foreign aid.

Under this alternative scenario, CBO projects annual war funding would decline from $58 billion in FY2015 to $30 billion in FY2017, and continue at that level for the rest of the decade. This estimate totals $340 billion in budget authority over 10 years, about half of the $646 billion in CBO's baseline estimate. CBO does not provide any additional details about the basis for its war cost estimate, which averages about $1 million per troop (**Table 13**).

CRS Analysis

Another way to analyze future war costs is to build from the "bottom up" by looking at the following key factors that affected Iraq withdrawal costs, particularly

- the number and cost of U.S. troops who remain in Afghanistan to train and support Afghan forces and conduct counter-terror operations;
- the extent of the decline in U.S. troops in the region providing regional support;
- the scope of reset/reconstitution after FY2015; and
- the U.S. contribution to the cost of supporting Afghan security forces.

Assuming that U.S. troop levels in Afghanistan decline as the President has announced, the cost of in- country forces could decline from $11 billion in the FY2015 request to about $1 billion in FY2017.[208] If the number of troops providing in-theater presence declines by about 25% based on the Iraq experience, then those costs could decline from $18 billion now to about $11 billion by FY2019.[209]

Another post-withdrawal cost could be reset expenses for two to three years after U.S. troops leave. Based on the Iraq experience, reset costs may fall rapidly once U.S. troops leave from $9.0 billion in the FY2015 request to $4.0 billion in FY2016 and $2.0 billion in FY2015.

Helping to pay for Afghan security forces could be another long-term cost. While the United States has not committed to specific funding amounts, both the 2012 Strategic Partnership Agreement and the NATO Wales summit communique this year call for ISAF nations "to contribute significantly" to sustaining Afghan security forces" through "the decade of transformation." [210] U.S. defense officials have estimated this commitment at $4.0 billion annually as long as the Afghan forces remain at current levels.

Taking these factors and historical experience into account, this CRS analysis suggests that U.S. war costs could fall from the $58 billion request in FY2015 to about $25 billion in FY2016 and then gradually decline to $20 billion in FY2017 and $15 billion for the rest of the decade.

Congressional Options to Affect Military Operations

In light of the new U.S. operation against the Islamic State, as well as some uncertainty about the nature of continued U.S. operations during the last stages of withdrawal from Afghanistan, Congress has voted on several amendments designed to place limits on military operations. Some concerns have been raised in response to recent press reports, saying that the President is permitting the military to broaden its mission to support Afghan security forces after December 2014 from "train and assist" to include air support and airstrikes in support of Afghan combat missions and in some circumstances, to accompany Afghan forces in ground operations against the Taliban.[211]

In drafting such amendments, Congress has turned to experience from Vietnam, Cambodia, and Iraq to look for options. In the past, Congress has considered both funding and non-funding options. Most observers would maintain that restrictions tied to appropriations have been more effective.[212] Restrictive funding options generally prohibit the obligation or expenditure of current or previously appropriated funds for certain purposes. Obligations occur when the government pays military or civilian personnel, or the services sign contracts or place orders to buy goods or services. Expenditures, or outlays, take place when payment is provided.

The Vietnam Experience

Past attempts or provisions to restrict funding have followed several patterns, including those that cut off funding

- for particular types of military activities but permit funding for other activities (e.g., prohibiting funds for combat activities but permitting funds to withdraw troops);
- as of a certain date in a specific country;
- "at the earliest practical date," which essentially gives the president leeway to set the date; or

- if certain conditions are met (such as a new authorization) or certain events take place (such as the release of U.S. prisoners of war).

Other non-funding approaches to restrict military operations have

- required that troops be withdrawn by a specified date or at the "earliest practical date";
- withdrawn funds unless there was a declaration of war or a specific congressional authorization of war; or
- repealed previous congressional resolutions authorizing military activities.

One or both houses may also state a "sense of the Congress," or non-binding resolution that does not need to be signed by the President, that U.S. military operations should be limited, wound down, or ended or forces withdrawn.

While only a handful of provisions have been enacted, congressional consideration of these various limiting provisions did place pressure on the Administration at the time, influencing the course of events. For example, the well-known Cooper-Church provision that prohibited the introduction of U.S. ground troops into Cambodia was enacted in early 1971 after U.S. forces had invaded and then been withdrawn from Cambodia. That provision was intended to prevent the reintroduction of troops.[213] Although President Nixon did not reintroduce U.S. troops, the United States continued to bomb Cambodia for the next three years.

Later in 1973, Congress passed two provisions that prohibited the obligation or expenditures of "any funds in this or any previous law on or after August 15, 1973" for combat "in or over or from off the shores of North Vietnam, South Vietnam, Laos, or Cambodia."[214] The final version of that provision reflected negotiations between the Administration and Congress about when the prohibition would go into effect, with August 15, 1973, set in the enacted version. Bombing did, in fact, stop on that day.

Several well-known proposals that were not enacted—two McGovern-Hatfield amendments and an earlier Cooper-Church amendment—were also part of this Vietnam-era jockeying between the Administration and Congress. One McGovern-Hatfield amendment prohibited expenditure of previously appropriated funds after a specified date "in or over Indochina," except for the purpose of withdrawing troops or protecting our Indochinese allies, while another also prohibited spending funds to support more than a specified number of troops unless the president notified the Congress of the need for a 60-day extension. The earlier Cooper-Church amendment prohibited the expenditure of any funds after July 1, 1970, to retain troops in Cambodia "unless specifically authorized by law hereafter."[215]

Generally, Congress continued to provide funds for U.S. troops in Vietnam at the requested levels as the Nixon Administration reduced troop levels. Overall, funding restrictions, it might be said, have generally proven more effective than the War Powers Act, which has been challenged by the executive branch on constitutional grounds.[216]

Restrictions Proposed More Recently

During the current Congress, the House voted on the following resolutions and amendments that would place limits on military operations in Iraq, Afghanistan, or Syria:

- H.Con.Res. 105 prohibits the President from deploying or maintaining U.S. armed forces in a sustained combat role in Iraq without specific, subsequent statutory authorization (passed House July 25, 2014);[217]
- H.Amdt. 928 to H.R. 4870, the FY2015 DOD Appropriations Act, provided that none of the funds in this act may be used to conduct combat operations in Afghanistan after December 31, 2014 (defeated 153-260, June 19, 2014);[218]
- H.Amdt. 914 to H.R. 4870 stated that "None of the funds made available in this Act may be used to provide man-portable air defense systems to Syria" (agreed to by voice vote, June 19, 2014).[219]
- H.Amdt. 917 to H.R. 4870 stated that none of the funds in Act "may be used to provide weapons in Syria" (defeated 167-244, June 19, 2014).[220]

In the 112th Congress, before President Obama announced the most recent troop withdrawal plan for Afghanistan, amendments were considered to limit funds to withdrawal costs:

- H.Amdt. 1103 to H.R. 4310, the FY2013National Defense Authorization Act, limited war funding in the act to paying for the safe and orderly withdrawal of U.S. troops and military contractors from Afghanistan (failed 113-303, May 17, 2012);[221]

- H.Amdt. 330 to H.R. 1540, the FY2012 National Defense Authorization Act required DOD to begin a "safe, responsible, and phased withdrawal" of U.S. ground troops except for small, counter-terrorism units (defeated 123-294, May 25, 2011).[222]

During the House debate over the FY2010 Supplemental (H.R. 4899), three amendments were voted on to restrict funding or troop levels for the Afghan war, similar to Vietnam-era amendments:

- H.Amdt. 3 would have deleted all military funding for the Afghan war (defeated 25-376);[223]
- H.Amdt. 4 would have limited the obligation and expenditure of funds to the protection and "safe and orderly withdrawal from Afghanistan of all members of the Armed Forces and Department of Defense contractor personnel who are in Afghanistan" (defeated 100-321);[224] and
- H.Amdt. 5 would have required the President to submit a plan for a "safe, orderly, and expeditious redeployment of the Armed Forces from Afghanistan," along with a "timetable for the completion of that redeployment and information regarding variables that could alter that timetable," as well as require that none of the funds in the act be obligated or expended "in a manner that is inconsistent with the President's policy announced on December 1, 2009, to begin the orderly withdrawal of United States troops from Afghanistan after July 1, 2011," unless the Congress approves a joint resolution that would receive expedited consideration in both houses (defeated 162-260). [225]

Appendix A. U.S. Troop Levels in Afghanistan and Iraq, FY2001-FY2015

Table A-1 shows monthly U.S. troops deployed in-country in Afghanistan and in Iraq from January 2002-September 2014 based on reports prepared by the Joint Staff and provided to Congress and CRS.[226] Beginning in May 2008, DOD began to include the total number of U.S. troops deployed not only in-country but also in the surrounding area to provide in-theater support, as well as those conducting other counterterror operations.

Table A-1. Boots on the Ground for Afghanistan/Operation Enduring Freedom and Iraq/ Operation Iraqi Freedom and Operation New Dawn December 2001-September 2014

	Jan.	Feb.	Mar.	Apr.	May	Jun.	Jul.	Aug.	Sep.	Oct.	Nov.	Dec.
2001: Afghanistan: Operation Enduring Freedom (OEF)												
										na	na	na
										na	na	na
OEF TOTAL										**na**	**na**	**na**
2001: Iraq: Operation Iraqi Freedom (OIF) and Operation New Dawn (OND)												
In-Country										0	0	0
In-Theater Support										na	na	na
OIF/OND TOTAL										***na***	***na***	***na***
2001: Totals: OEF, OIF/OND												
										na	na	na
In-Theater Support										na	na	na
OEF & OIF/OND Total										**na**	**na**	**na**
2002: OEF												
	4,100	4,200	5,000	6,600	6,900	7,300	8,900	9,500	10,400	10,500	10,200	9,700
	Jan.	**Feb.**	**Mar.**	**Apr.**	**May**	**Jun.**	**Jul.**	**Aug.**	**Sep.**	**Oct.**	**Nov.**	**Dec.**
	na	na	na	na	na	na	na	na	na	na	na	na
OEF Total	**na**	**na**	**na**	**na**	**na**	**na**	**na**	**na**	**na**	**na**	**na**	**na**

Table A-1. (Continued)

	Jan.	Feb.	Mar.	Apr.	May	Jun.	Jul.	Aug.	Sep.	Oct.	Nov.	Dec.
2002: OIF/OND												
In-Country	0	0	0	0	0	0	0	0	0	0	0	0
In-Theater Support	na	na	na	na	na	na	na	na	na	na	na	na
OIF/OND Total	***na***	***na***	***na***	***na***	***na***	***na***	***na***	***na***	***na***	***na***	***na***	***na***
2002: Totals: OEF, OIF/OND												
	4,100	4,200	5,000	6,600	6,900	7,300	8,900	9,500	10,400	10,500	10,200	9,700
In-Theater Support	na	na	na	na	na	na	na	na	na	na	na	na
OEF & OIF/OND Total	**na**	**na**	**na**	**na**	**na**	**na**	**na**	**na**	**na**	**na**	**na**	**na**
2003: OEF												
In-Country	9,800	9,500	11,450	9,300	9,900	10,900	10,900	12,700	9,800	12,100	12,000	13,100
In-Theater Support	na	na	na	na	na	na	na	na	na	na	na	na
OEF Total	***9,800***	***9,500***	***11,450***	***9,300***	***9,900***	***10,900***	***10,900***	***12,700***	***9,800***	***12,100***	***12,000***	***13,100***
2003: OIF/OND												
In-Country	0	0	0	93,900	145,700	147,400	149,400	146,000	130,300	136,900	131,300	123,700
In-Theater Support	na	na	na	na	na	na	na	na	na	na	na	na
OIF/OND Total	**na**	**na**	**na**	**na**	**na**	**na**	**na**	**na**	**na**	**na**	**na**	**na**
2003: Totals: OEF, OIF/OND												
	9,800	9,500	11,450	103,200	155,600	158,300	160,300	158,700	140,100	149,000	143,300	136,800
In-Theater Support	na	na	na	na	na	na	na	na	na	na	na	na

	Jan.	Feb.	Mar.	Apr.	May	Jun.	Jul.	Aug.	Sep.	Oct.	Nov.	Dec.
OEF & OIF/OND Total	**na**	**na**	**na**	**na**	**na**	**na**	**na**	**na**	**na**	**na**	**na**	**na**
2004: OEF												
	13,500	12,300	14,100	19,500	17,700	17,800	17,400	15,700	16,800	17,500	15,765	18,300
	na	na	na	na	na	na	na	na	na	na	na	na
	Jan.	**Feb.**	**Mar.**	**Apr.**	**May**	**Jun.**	**Jul.**	**Aug.**	**Sep.**	**Oct.**	**Nov.**	**Dec.**
OEF Total	**na**	**na**	**na**	**na**	**na**	**na**	**na**	**na**	**na**	**na**	**na**	**na**
2004: OIF/OND												
In-Country	126,900	108,400	119,600	131,700	139,800	144,300	140,600	126,800	137,700	134,600	132,837	142,600
In-Theater Support	na	na	na	na	na	na	na	na	na	na	na	na
OIF/OND Total	**na**	**na**	**na**	**na**	**na**	**na**	**na**	**na**	**na**	**na**	**na**	**na**
2004: Totals: OEF, OIF/OND												
	140,400	120,700	133,700	151,200	157,500	162,100	158,000	142,500	154,500	152,100	148,602	160,900
In-Theater Support	na	na	na	na	na	na	na	na	na	na	na	na
OEF & OIF/OND Total	**na**	**na**	**na**	**na**	**na**	**na**	**na**	**na**	**na**	**na**	**na**	**na**
2005: OEF												
	17,222	20,300	19,409	18,991	19,044	19,200	17,836	17,833	17,830	17,827	17,824	17,821
	na	na	na	na	na	na	na	na	na	na	na	na
OEF Total	**na**	**na**	**na**	**na**	**na**	**na**	**na**	**na**	**na**	**na**	**na**	**na**
2005: OIF/OND												
In-Country	150,682	161,200	144,875	144,776	137,157	141,100	136,475	140,776	145,078	149,379	153,681	157,982

Table A-1. (Continued)

	Jan.	Feb.	Mar.	Apr.	May	Jun.	Jul.	Aug.	Sep.	Oct.	Nov.	Dec.
In-Theater Support	na	na	na	na	na	na	na	na	na	na	na	na
OIF/OND Total	**na**	**na**	**na**	**na**	**na**	**na**	**na**	**na**	**na**	**na**	**na**	**na**
2005: Totals: OEF, OIF/OND												
	167,904	181,500	164,284	163,767	156,201	160,300	154,311	158,609	162,908	167,206	171,505	175,803
In-Theater Support	na	na	na	na	na	na	na	na	na	na	na	na
OEF & OIF/OND Total	**na**	**na**	**na**	**na**	**na**	**na**	**na**	**na**	**na**	**na**	**na**	**na**
2006: OEF												
	18,457	20,297	22,528	21,845	22,990	21,733	22,103	20,764	18,611	19,090	19,791	20,502
	na	na	na	na	na	na	na	na	na	na	na	na
OEF Total	**na**	**na**	**na**	**na**	**na**	**na**	**na**	**na**	**na**	**na**	**na**	**na**
2006: OIF/OND												
In-Country	153,239	137,365	129,713	129,467	130,231	128,789	124,876	131,057	140,264	139,421	147,796	133,718
In-Theater Support	na	na	na	na	na	na	na	na	na	na	na	na
OIF/OND Total	***153,239***	***137,365***	***129,713***	***129,467***	***130,231***	***128,789***	***124,876***	***131,057***	***140,264***	***139,421***	***147,796***	***133,718***
2006: Totals: OEF, OIF/OND												
	171,696	157,662	152,341	151,312	153,221	150,522	146,979	151,821	158,875	158,511	167,587	154,220
In-Theater Support	na	na	na	na	na	na	na	na	na	na	na	na
OEF & OIF/OND Total	**na**	**na**	**na**	**na**	**na**	**na**	**na**	**na**	**na**	**na**	**na**	**na**

	Jan.	Feb.	Mar.	Apr.	May	Jun.	Jul.	Aug.	Sep.	Oct.	Nov.	Dec.
2007: OEF												
In-Country	20,947	25,876	24,842	24,310	24,060	26,480	23,881	24,008	24,056	24,615	24,474	24,780
In-Theater Support	na	na	na	na	na	na	na	na	na	na	na	na
OEF Total	**na**	**na**	**na**	**na**	**na**	**na**	**na**	**na**	**na**	**na**	**na**	**na**
2007: OIF/OND												
In-Country	128,569	134,754	137,976	144,486	144,202	150,336	156,247	157,674	165,607	164,353	164,424	161,783
In-Theater Support	na	na	na	na	na	na	na	na	na	na	na	na
OIF/OND Total	**na**	**na**	**na**	**na**	**na**	**na**	**na**	**na**	**na**	**na**	**na**	**na**
2007: Totals: OEF, OIF/OND												
	149,516	160,630	162,818	168,796	168,262	176,816	180,128	181,682	189,663	188,968	188,898	186,563
In-Theater Support	na	na	na	na	na	na	na	na	na	na	na	na
OEF & OIF/OND Total	**na**	**na**	**na**	**na**	**na**	**na**	**na**	**na**	**na**	**na**	**na**	**na**
2008: OEF												
	26,607	28,050	28,650	33,000	35,602	33,902	33,600	34,200	33,750	33,125	32,813	32,500
	na	na	na	na	13,398	14,348	13,500	13,300	13,350	12,925	12,713	12,500
OEF Total	**na**	**na**	**na**	**na**	***49,000***	***48,250***	***47,100***	***47,500***	***47,100***	***46,050***	***45,525***	***45,000***
2008: OIF/OND												
In-Country	155,846	158,400	159,700	162,400	158,900	153,300	147,400	145,000	146,900	147,700	148,100	148,500
In-Theater Support	na	na	na	na	33,950	28,760	32,100	27,900	35,400	33,250	32,175	31,100
OIF/OND Total	**na**	**na**	**na**	**na**	***192,850***	***182,060***	***179,500***	***172,900***	***182,300***	***180,950***	***180,275***	***179,600***

Table A-1. (Continued)

	Jan.	Feb.	Mar.	Apr.	May	Jun.	Jul.	Aug.	Sep.	Oct.	Nov.	Dec.
2008: Totals: OEF, OIF/OND												
	182,453	186,450	188,350	195,400	194,502	187,202	181,000	179,200	180,650	180,825	180,913	181,000
In-Theater Support	na	na	na	na	47,348	43,108	45,600	41,200	48,750	46,175	44,888	43,600
OEF & OIF/OND Total	**na**	**na**	**na**	**na**	**241,850**	**230,310**	**226,600**	**220,400**	**229,400**	**227,000**	**225,800**	**224,600**
2009: OEF												
	32,800	35,900	38,350	39,000	44,600	55,100	56,500	62,600	62,300	65,800	67,500	69,000
	13,600	13,200	13,950	15,200	13,800	14,600	14,400	14,500	16,300	15,400	15,400	15,500
OEF Total	***46,400***	***49,100***	***52,300***	***54,200***	***58,400***	***69,700***	***70,900***	***77,100***	***78,600***	***81,200***	***82,900***	***84,500***
2009: OIF/OND												
In-Country	147,700	146,400	141,300	139,400	134,200	134,500	132,300	132,600	129,200	120,300	119,700	114,300
In-Theater Support	25,400	29,300	27,450	26,400	30,000	28,000	27,700	30,800	31,400	29,700	29,100	28,500
OIF/OND Total	***173,100***	***175,700***	***168,750***	***165,800***	***164,200***	***162,500***	***160,000***	***163,400***	***160,600***	***150,000***	***148,800***	***142,800***
2009: Totals: OEF, OIF/OND												
	180,500	182,300	179,650	178,400	178,800	189,600	188,800	195,200	191,500	186,100	187,200	183,300
In-Theater Support	39,000	42,500	41,400	41,600	43,800	42,600	42,100	45,300	47,700	45,100	44,500	44,000
OEF & OIF/OND Total	**219,500**	**224,800**	**221,050**	**220,000**	**222,600**	**232,200**	**230,900**	**240,500**	**239,200**	**231,200**	**231,700**	**227,300**
2010: OEF												
	70,200	74,600	79 100	87,600	89,700	93,800	89,300	90,800	96,600	96,200	97,600	96,900
	15,400	16,200	2 200	3,200	16,700	17,800	25,600	26,700	25,000	28,300	31,600	26,800

	Jan.	Feb.	Mar.	Apr.	May	Jun.	Jul.	Aug.	Sep.	Oct.	Nov.	Dec.
OEF Total	***85,600***	***90,800***	***81,300***	***90,800***	***106,400***	***111,600***	***114,900***	***117,500***	***121,600***	***124,500***	***129,200***	***123,700***
	Jan.	**Feb.**	**Mar.**	**Apr.**	**May**	**Jun.**	**Jul.**	**Aug.**	**Sep.**	**Oct.**	**Nov.**	**Dec.**
2010: OIF/OND												
In-Country	112,400	101,100	95,900	98,850	94,250	88,320	80,620	60,710	48,810	47,810	48,410	47,305
In-Theater Support	30,000	28,500	27,400	29,100	27,000	27,610	27,110	37,410	35,520	36,010	39,000	42,100
OIF/OND Total	***142,400***	***129,600***	***123,300***	***127,950***	***121,250***	***115,930***	***107,730***	***98,120***	***84,330***	***83,820***	***87,410***	***89,405***
2010: Totals: OEF, OIF/OND												
	182,600	175,700	175,000	186,450	183,950	182,120	169,920	151,510	145,410	144,010	146,010	144,205
In-Theater Support	45,400	44,700	29,600	32,300	43,700	45,410	52,710	64,110	60,520	64,310	70,600	68,900
OEF & OIF/OND Total	**228,000**	**220,400**	**204,600**	**218,750**	**227,650**	**227,530**	**222,630**	**215,620**	**205,930**	**208,320**	**216,610**	**213,105**
2011: OEF												
	96,700	99,500	99,800	99,300	99,500	98,900	98,500	98,100	98,200	97,800	97,700	94,100
	26,000	31,500	29,800	32,100	31,100	33,000	33,000	33,000	27,700	31,400	28,300	27,000
OEF Total	***122,700***	***131,000***	***129,600***	***131,400***	***130,600***	***131,900***	***131,500***	***131,100***	***125,900***	***129,200***	***126,000***	***121,100***
2011: OIF/OND												
In-Country	46,705	46,805	45,660	46,360	48,110	46,010	45,510	45,605	44,755	42,455	33,835	11,455
In-Theater Support	28,700	32,500	42,150	32,050	32,600	38,300	33,700	32,800	29,700	36,650	44,700	42,855
OIF/OND Total	***75,405***	***79,305***	***87,810***	***78,410***	***80,710***	***84,310***	***79,210***	***78,405***	***74,455***	***79,105***	***78,535***	***54,310***
2011: Totals: OEF, OIF/OND												
	143,405	146,305	145,460	145,660	147,610	144,910	144,010	143,705	142,955	140,255	131,535	105,555
In-Theater Support	54,700	64,000	71,950	64,150	63,700	71,300	66,700	65,800	57,400	68,050	73,000	69,855

Table A-1. (Continued)

	Jan.	Feb.	Mar.	Apr.	May	Jun.	Jul.	Aug.	Sep.	Oct.	Nov.	Dec.
OEF & OIF/OND Total	**198,105**	**210,305**	**217,410**	**209,810**	**211,310**	**216,210**	**210,710**	**209,505**	**200,355**	**208,305**	**204,535**	**175,410**
						2012: OEF						
	88,300	89,300	88,200	88,000	87,400	85,600	85,300	84,000	76,500	65,900	66,000	65,800
	67,900	68,800	68,300	69,900	69,000	70,900	66,200	66,600	68,800	72,700	69,900	68,500
OEF Total	***156,200***	***158,100***	***156,500***	***157,900***	***156,400***	***156,500***	***151,500***	***150,600***	***145,300***	***138,600***	***135,900***	***134,300***
						2012: OIF/OND						
Iraq In-Country	0	0	0	0	0	0	0	0	0	0	0	0
OIF In-Theater Support	0	0	0	0	0	0	0	0	0	0	0	0
OIF/OND Total	***0***	***0***	***0***	***0***	***0***	***0***	***0***	***0***	***0***	***0***	***0***	***0***
						2012: Totals: OEF, OIF/OND						
	88,300	89,300	88,200	88,000	87,400	85,600	85,300	84,000	76,500	65,900	66,000	65,800
	67,900	68,800	68,300	69,900	69,000	70,900	66,200	66,600	68,800	72,700	69,900	68,500
OEF & OIF/OND Total	**156,200**	**158,100**	**156,500**	**157,900**	**156,400**	**156,500**	**151,500**	**150,600**	**145,300**	**138,600**	**135,900**	**134,300**
						2013: OEF						
	65,300	66,800	65,700	63,500	63,500	61,300	60,000	60,900	55,800	51,200	48,000	43,300
	64,000	63,600	64,700	63,700	63,600	60,400	57,500	59,800	66,400	68,800	66,000	61,800
OEF Total	***129,300***	***130,400***	***130,400***	***127,200***	***127,100***	***121,700***	***117,500***	***120,700***	***122,200***	***120,000***	***114,000***	***105,100***
						2013: OIF/OND						
In-Country	0	0	0	0	0	0	0	0	0	0	0	0
In-Theater Support	0	0	0	0	0	0	0	0	0	0	0	0

	Jan.	Feb.	Mar.	Apr.	May	Jun.	Jul.	Aug.	Sep.	Oct.	Nov.	Dec.
OIF/OND Total	***0***	***0***	***0***	***0***	***0***	***0***	***0***	***0***	***0***	***0***	***0***	***0***
					2013: Totals: OEF, OIF/OND							
	65,300	66,800	65,700	63,500	63,500	61,300	60,000	60,900	55,800	51,200	48,000	43,300
In-Theater Support	64,000	63,600	64,700	63,700	63,600	60,400	57,500	59,800	66,400	68,800	66,000	61,800
OEF & OIF/OND Total	***129,300***	***130,400***	***130,400***	***127,200***	***127,100***	***121,700***	***117,500***	***120,700***	***122,200***	***120,000***	***114,000***	***105,100***
					2014: OEF							
	37,600	33,200	33,200	32,900	32,500							
	62,100	60,700	60,100	60,800	59,000							
OEF Total	***99,700***	***93,900***	***93,300***	***93,700***	***91,500***							
					2014: OIF/OND							
In-Country	0	0	0	0	0							
In-Theater Support	0	0	0	0	0							
OIF/OND Total	***0***	***0***	***0***	***0***	***0***							
					2014: Totals: OEF, OIF/OND							
	37,600	33,200	33,200	32,900	32,500	31,400	30,400	29,600	27,800			
In-Theater Support	62,100	60,700	60,100	60,800	59,000	56,200	57,200	58,000	57,100			
OEF and OIF/OND Total	***99,700***	***93,900***	***93,300***	***93,700***	***91,500***	***87,600***	***87,600***	***87,600***	***84,900***			

Source: CRS calculations from DOD, Joint Staff, Summary and Monthly Boots on the Ground Reports to Congress, as originally requested in H.Rept. 111-230 accompanying H.R. 3230, Department of Defense Appropriations Act, 2010. Boots on the Ground data first available in January 2002. Total by operation (OEF/OIF/OND) not available in Boots on the Ground Report until 2008.

Appendix B. OMB Criteria for War Costs

In February 2009, at the beginning of the Obama administration, OMB issued new budget guidance to DOD providing criteria for expenses to be considered as appropriate for war funding. Revised in September 2010 to clarify the distinctions, the letter states that the criteria "for deciding whether funding properly belongs in the base budget or in the budget for overseas contingency operations (OCO) ... have been very successful in delineating between these two sources of funding," according to OMB (see below).[227]

September 9, 2010

The Honorable Robert Hale
Under Secretary of Defense (Comptroller) 1100Defense Pentagon
Washington, D.C. 20301-1100

Dear Mr. Hale:

In early 2009 OMB and the Department developed criteria for deciding whether funding properly belongs in the base budget or in the budget for overseas contingency operations (OCO). These criteria have been very successful in delineating between these two sources of funding and have facilitated the development of coherent and defensible OCO funding requests. Since then, and in close collaboration with Comptroller representatives, we have developed updated criteria that build on our experience in the subsequent two budget cycles. This update clarifies language, eliminates areas of confusion and provides guidance for areas previously unanticipated.

The enclosure to this letter contains the updated criteria and replaces the 2009 criteria.

OMB will use these updated criteria when reviewing the Department's budget submissions.

We recognize that in developing these updated criteria several policy issues arose that remain unresolved. These will be addressed in the FY 2012 budget review.

Please contact. 202-395-3879 if you have any questions about these criteria

Sincerely,

Steven M. Kosiak Associate Director for Defense and Foreign Affairs

Table B-1. Criteria for War/Overseas Contingency Operations Funding Requests

Item	Definition of Criteria
Geographic area covered/"Theater of operations"(for non-classified war/overseas contingency operations funding)	Geographic areas in which combat or direct combat support operations occur: Iraq , Afghanistan, Pakistan, Kazakhstan, Tajikistan, Kyrgyzstan, the Horn of Africa, Persian Gulf and Gulf nations, Arabian Sea, the Indian Ocean, the Philippines, and other countries on a case-by-case basis. Note: OCO budget items must also meet the criteria below.
Inclusions	
Major Equipment (General)	Replacement of losses that have occurred but only for items not already programmed for replacement in the Future Years Defense Plan (FYDP)— no accelerations. Accelerations can be made in the base budget. Replacement or repair to original capability (to upgraded capability if that is currently available) of equipment returning from theater. The replacement may be a similar end item if the original item is no longer in production. Incremental cost of non-war related upgrades, if made, should be included in the base. Purchase of specialized, theater-specific equipment. Funding must be obligated within 12 months.
Ground Equipment Replacement	Combat losses and washouts (returning equipment that is not economical to repair); replacement of equipment given to coalition partners, if consistent with approved policy; in-theater stocks above customary eouipping levels on a case-bv-case basis.
Equipment Modifications (Enhancements)	Operationally required modifications to equipment used in theater or in direct support of combat operations, for which funding can be obligated in 12 months, and that is not already programmed in FYDP.

Table B-1. (Continued)

Item	Definition of Criteria
Munitions	Replenishment of munitions expended in combat operations in theater. Training ammunition for theater-unique training events is allowed. Forecasted expenditures are not allowed. Case-by-case assessment for munitions where existing stocks are insufficient to sustain theater combat operations.
Aircraft Replacement	Combat losses, defined as losses by accident or by enemy action that occur in the theater of ooerations.
Military Construction	Facilities and infrastructure in the theater of operations in direct support of combat operations. The level of construction should be the minimum to meet operational requirements. At non-enduring locations, facilities and infrastructure for temporary use are covered. At enduring locations, construction requirements must be tied to surge operations or major changes in operational requirements and will be considered on a case-by-case basis.
Research and Development	Projects required for combat operations in these specific theaters that can be delivered in 12 months.
Operations	Direct War costs: • transport of personnel, equipment, and supplies to, from, and within the theater of operations; • deployment-specific training and preparation for units and personnel (military and civilian) to assume their directed missions as defined in the orders for deployment into the theater of operations; Within the theater, the incremental costs above the funding programmed in the base budget: • to support commanders in the conduct of their directed missions (to include Emergency Response Programs); • to build and maintain temporary facilities; • to provide food, fuel, supplies. contracted services and other support; and

Item	Definition of Criteria
	• to cover the operational costs of coalition partners supporting U.S. military missions, as mutually agreed. Indirect War Costs: Indirect war costs incurred outside the theater of operations will be evaluated on a case-by-case basis.
Health	Short-term care directly related to combat. Infrastructure that is only to be used during the current conflict.
Personnel (Incremental Pay)	Incremental special pays and allowances for Service members and civilians deployed to a combat zone; incremental pay. special pays and allowances for Reserve Component personnel mobilized to support war missions.
Special Operations Command	Operations and equipment that meet the criteria in this guidance.
Prepositioned Supplies and Equipment	Resetting in-theater stocks of supplies and equipment to pre-war levels. Excludes costs for reconfiguring prepositioned sets or for maintaining them.
Security Force Funding	Training, equipping, and sustaining Iraqi and Afghan military and police forces.
Fuel	War fuel costs, and funding to ensure that logistical support to combat operations is not degraded due to cash losses in DoD's baseline fuel program. Would fund enough of any base fuel shortfall attributable to fuel price increases to maintain sufficient on-hand cash for the Defense Working Capital Funds to cover seven days' disbursements. (This would enable the Fund to partially cover losses attributable to fuel cost increases.)
Exclusions. From war/overseas contingency funding! - Appropriately funded in the base budget	
Training equipment	Training vehicles, aircraft, ammunition, and simulators. Exception: training base stocks of specialized, theater-specific equipment that is required to support combat operations in the theater of operations, and support to deployment-specific training described above.

Table B-1. (Continued)

Item	Definition of Criteria
Equipment Service Life	Acceleration of SLEPs already in the FYDP.
Extension Programs (SLEPs)	
Base Realignment and Closure (BRAC)	BRAC projects.
Family Support Initiatives	Family support initiatives to include the construction of childcare facilities; funding private-public partnerships to expand military families' access to childcare; and support for service members' spouses professional development.
Industrial Base Capacity	Programs to maintain industrial base capacity (e.g. "war-stoooers").
Personnel	Recruiting and retention bonuses to maintain end-strength. Basic Pay and the Basic allowances for Housing and Subsistence for permanently authorized end strength. Individual augmentees will be decided on a case-by-case basis.
Office of Security Cooperation	Support for the personnel, operations, or the construction or maintenance of facilities, at U.S. Offices of Security Cooperation in-theater.
Special Situations	
Reprogrammings and paybacks	Items proposed for increases in reprogramrnings or as payback for prior reprogrammings must meet the criteria above.

Source: OMB.

APPENDIX C. WAR APPROPRIATIONS BY PUBLIC LAW AND AGENCY

The table below shows enacted appropriations by act from FY2001-FY2014.

Table C-1. Defense Department, Foreign Operations Funding, and VA Medical Funding for Iraq, Afghanistan, and Other Global War on Terror Activities, FY2001-FY2014 (in billions of dollars of budget authority)

Name of Law	Public Law Number	Date Enacted	DOD Funds	State/ USAID	VA Medical	Total cost
FY2001 Emerg. Supp. Approp. Act for Recovery from and Response to Terrorist Attacks on the United States	P.L. 107-38	9/18/01	13.6	0.3	0	13.9
FY2002 Dept. of Defense and Emergency Terrorism Response Act	P.L. 107-117	1/10/02	3.4	0	0	3.4
FY2002 Emergency Supplemental	P.L. 107-206	8/2/02	13.8	0.4	0	14.1
FY2002 Regular Foreign Operations	P.L. 107-115	1/10/02	0.0	0.2	0	0.2
FY2003 Consolidated Appropriations	P.L. 108-7	2/20/03	10.0	0.4	0	10.4
FY2003 Emergency Supplemental	P.L. 108-11	4/16/03	62.6	3.4	0	66.0
FY2003 DOD Appropriations[a]	P.L. 107-248	10/23/02	7.1	0	0	7.1
FY2004 DOD Appropriations Act[a]	P.L. 108-87	9/30/03	-3.5	0	0	-3.5
FY2004 Emergency Supplemental	P.L. 108-106	11/6/03	64.9	21.2	0	86.1
FY2004 Foreign Operations Appropriations	P.L. 108-199	1/23/04	0	0.5	0	0.5
FY2005 DOD Appropriations Act[b]	P.L. 108-287	8/5/04	25.0	0.7	0	25.7
FY2005 DOD Appropriations Act	P.L. 108-287	8/5/04	2.1	0	0	2.1

Table C-1. (Continued)

Name of Law	Public Law Number	Date Enacted	DOD Funds	State/ USAID	VA Medical	Total cost
FY2005 Consolidated Approps.	P.L. 108-447	12/8/04	0	1.0	0	1.0
FY2005 Supplemental Approps.[c]	P.L. 109-13	5/11/05	75.9	3.1	0	79.0
FY2006 Interior and Rel. Ag. Approps.[d]	P.L. 109-54	8/2/05	0	0	0.2	0.2
FY2006 Foreign Operations Approps.	P.L. 109-102	11/14/05	0	1.0	0	1.0
FY2006 Science, State, and Rel. Agencies Appropriations Act	P.L. 109-108	11/22/05	0	0.1	0	0.1
FY2006 Military Quality of Life and Veterans Affairs[d]	P.L. 109-114	11/30/05	0	0	0.4	0.4
FY2006 DOD Approps Act	P.L. 109-148	12/30/05	50.0	0	0	50.0
FY2006 DOD Appropriations Act	P.L. 109-148	12/30/05	0.8	0	0	0.8
FY2006 Emergency Supplemental	P.L. 109-234	6/15/06	66.0	3.2	0	69.2
FY2007 DOD Appropriations Act[e]	P.L. 109-289	9/29/06	70.5	0	0	70.5
FY2007 Continuing Resolution[f]	P.L. 110-5	2/15/07	0	1.3	0.6	1.8
FY2007 Supplemental	P.L. 110-28	5/25/07	94.5	3.8	0.4	98.7
FY2008 Continuing Resolution	P.L. 110-92	9/29/07	5.2	0	0	5.2
FY2008 DOD Appropriations Act	P.L. 110-116	11/13/07	11.6	0	0	11.6
FY2008 Consolidated Approps. Act	P.L. 110-161	12/26/07	70.0	2.3	0.9	73.2
FY2008 Supplemental Approps. Act[g]	P.L. 110-252	6/30/08	157.9	5.0	0.4	163.2
FY2009 Consolidated Security, Disaster Assistance, and	P.L. 110-329	9/30/08	2.5	0	1.5	4.0

Name of Law	Public Law Number	Date Enacted	DOD Funds	State/ USAID	VA Medical	Total cost
Continuing Appropriations Act						
FY2009 Omnibus Appropriations Act	P.L. 111-8	3/11/09	0	1.1	0	1.1
FY2009 Supplemental Appropriations Act	P.L. 111-32	6/24/09	80.0	2.5	0	82.5
FY2010 Consolidated Appropriations Act	P.L. 111-117	12/16/09	1.4	4.8	2.0	8.2
FY2010 DOD Appropriations Act, Title IX	P.L. 111-118	12/19/09	127.3	0	0	127.3
FY2010 Supplemental	P.L. 111-212	7/27/10	30.8	3.4	0	34.2
FY2011 Defense Appropriations and Full Year Continuing Resolution	P.L. 112-10	4/15/11	158.9	5.4	2.3	166.5
FY2012 Consolidated Appropriations Act	P.L. 112-74	12/23/11	115.2	11.5	2.9	129.6
FY2013 Consolidated and Continuing Appropriations Act Post-sequester	P.L. 113-6	3/26/13	82.1	9.2	3.2	94.5
FY2014 Consolidated Appropriations Act	P.L. 113-76 1	1/17/14	85.3	6.0	3.7	95.0

Sources: CRS calculations based on public laws, reports, explanatory statements, and DOD documents.

Notes: NA = Not applicable. Numbers may not add to totals due to rounding. DOD's regular appropriations bills included a separate Title IX for additional emergency appropriations for war costs from FY2005-FY2010 to "bridge" the gap between the beginning of the fiscal year and passage of a supplemental.

a. FY2003 Appropriations Act included $7.1 billion in regular FY2003 defense appropriations for GWOT that DOD cannot track; the FY2004 DOD Appropriations Act rescinded $3.5 billion in FY2003 war monies.

b. Reflects funds obligated for Operation Noble Eagle from DOD's regular appropriations as reported by the Defense Finance Accounting Service.

c. Excludes funds for Tsunami relief.

d. Includes VA medical funds for Iraq and Afghan veterans in emergency funding in Interior bill and in regular VA appropriations.

e. Title IX funds in FY2005 do not include a $1.8 billion scoring adjustment that reverses the previous rescission of FY2004 funds because this did not change wartime monies.
f. State Department figures for foreign and diplomatic operations; CRS estimates for VA medical.
g. The FY2008 Supplemental included funds for both FY2008 and bridge funds for FY2009.

APPENDIX D. WAR FUNDING BY FUNCTION, FY2009-FY2015

Since FY2009, DOD has provided a functional breakdown of war costs, which helps to compare changes in troop levels and changes in war costs. The categories range from operational costs to coalition support.[228] **Table D-1** combines these elements into three major categories:

- *Operational*, including operations, force protection, in-theater support, military intelligence, and military construction, largely reflecting troop levels;
- *Investment*, including reset or reconstitution that pays for repairing and replacing war-worn equipment reflecting the extent and pace of operations as well as changing definitions of war costs;
- *Programmatic* support, covering training of Afghan and Iraq security forces, coalition support, and other supporting activities not necessarily related to changes in troop strength.
- *Other costs*, including national intelligence and activities with little, if any, relationship to war operations.[229]

Operational Costs and Troop Levels

While overall costs may not rise or fall with troop levels, operational costs would be expected to change roughly proportionately. In the case of Iraq, both overall and operational costs fell by about 90%, in line with troop strength. As troop strength fell from 140,000 in FY2009 to 9,180 in FY2012, overall funding fell from $89.1 billion in FY2009 to $9.6 billion in FY2012 when all U.S. troops were out of Iraq (**Table D-1**).

In the case of the Afghan drawdown, neither overall nor operational costs have fallen proportionately since the FY2011 peak in strength. As of the FY2015 request, average strength is slated to fall by 88% and total cost by 56% since that peak. While operational costs would fall slightly faster, by 62%, the decline lags decreases in troop strength. DOD has suggested that operational costs remain high because of the need to dismantle bases and dispose of equipment as troop levels fall as would also have been the case in Iraq.

One source of the disparity between Afghanistan and Iraq may be the $18 billion cost for over 60,000 U.S. troops currently providing in-theater support. While the number of in-theater support troops declined as U.S. troops left Iraq, some troops in neighboring countries like Kuwait remained and their cost was allocated to OEF (**Figure 2**). In FY2015, DOD projects an increase in these support troop levels to 63,000. The persistence of these support troops raises the question of whether the cost of these troops is more appropriately considered an "enduring" cost that could transition into DOD's base budget.

Reset—repair or replacing war-worn equipment—costs in Afghanistan are projected to remain high during the withdrawal, increasing from $8.4 billion in FY2014 to 9.2 billion in FY2015, unlike the Iraq experience when these costs fell rapidly from $8.9 billion in FY2011 to $1.6 billion in FY2012 (**Table D-1**). While DOD may argue that more equipment may have accumulated in Afghanistan over the past 13 years of war, these high levels of funding for reset could also reflect "forward financing," or providing funds before the work can be executed by the depots.[230]

Based on Army budget repair plans—and the bulk of equipment returned from Afghanistan goes to Army depots—the amount of orders estimated to carry over from one fiscal year to the next is expected to be $3.5 billion in FY2014 and $2.9 billion in FY2015. Both these levels exceed DOD criteria for appropriate carryover levels.[231] In the past, Congress has reduced funding when carryover levels are high, questioning whether plans can be executed.

As would be expected, operational costs make up the bulk of war costs in both the Afghan and Iraq war, generally an average of 65% in Afghanistan and over 70% in Iraq. The share for reset in Iraq rose as equipment was more heavily used and as the definition of war expense broadened, and then decreased as the definition narrowed and equipment was used less heavily as the U.S. mission shifted to "train and assist," and the number of troops fell. The FY2015 request for Afghanistan does not follow this pattern.

Table D-1. Functional Breakdown for the Afghan and Iraq Wars FY2009-FY2015 Request in Billions of Dollars

By Category Fiscal Year	Afghan War/OEF							Iraq War/OIF and OND						
	2009	2010	2011	2012	2013	2014	2015	2009	2010	2011	2012	2013	2014	2015
Average Troop Strength and Cost from Peak: 2011= Afghanistan, 2009 = Iraq														
In-Country Strength	43,800	84,000	98,350	89,450	62,760	37,320	11,660	140,160	96,000	46,570	9,180	0	0	0
Change since peak in														
Troop Strength	**na**	**na**	**0%**	**-9%**	**-36%**	**-62%**	**-88%**	**0%**	**-32%**	**-67%**	**-93%**	**- 100%**	**-100%**	**-100%**
Total Cost	**na**	**na**	**0%**	**-7%**	**-25%**	**-38%**	**-56%**	**0%**	**-31%**	**-49%**	**-89%**	**-96%**	**-99%**	**-100%**
Operational Cost	**na**	**na**	**0%**	**-13%**	**-27%**	**-39%**	**-62%**	**0%**	**-30%**	**-55%**	**-89%**	**- 100%**	**-100%**	**-100%**
Operational Costs in Billions of $														
Operations/Force Protection[c]	23.9	55.0	58.2	54.1	27.6	26.2	11.2	52.4	37.5	26.9	6.5	0	0	0
In-Theater Support[d]	ns	ns	ns	ns	22.8	19.8	17.9	ns	ns	ns	ns	0.1	0.1	0.1
Force Protection[e]	4.7	11.4	10.3	6.1	ns	ns	ns	9.6	7.3	1.4	0.5	ns	ns	ns
Military Intelligence	1.9	4.9	6.1	5.5	4.4	ns	ns	3.0	1.0	0.8	0.3	0	ns	ns
Military Construction	0.9	2.0	1.2	0.3	0.2	0.0	ns	0.1	0	0	0	0	0	0
Subtotal: Operational	**31.4**	**73.3**	**75.8**	**65.9**	**55.0**	**46.0**	**29.2**	**65.0**	**45.8**	**29.1**	**7.3**	**0.1**	**0.1**	**0.1**
Equipment Reset and Reconstitution Costs in Billions of $														
Reset Equipment and Reconstit.	6.6	8.2	12.7	11.3	9.9	8.4	9.2	16.5	8.5	8.9	1.6	1.2	0.5	0.0
Subtotal: Reset	**6.6**	**8.2**	**12.7**	**11.3**	**9.9**	**8.4**	**9.2**	**16.5**	**8.5**	**8.9**	**1.6**	**1.2**	**0.5**	**0.0**
Programmatic Support Costs in Billions of $														
IED Defeat	0.7	0.9	2.4	2.4	1.6	0.9	0.4	2.7	0.9	0.4	0	0	0	0

By Category Fiscal Year	Afghan War/OEF							Iraq War/OIF and OND						
	2009	2010	2011	2012	2013	2014	2015	2009	2010	2011	2012	2013	2014	2015
Iraq Security Forces Fd.	0	0	0	0	0	0	0	1.0	1.0	1.5	0	0	0	0
Afghan Security Forces Fd.	5.6	9.2	11.6	11.2	5.1	4.7	4.1	0	0	0	0	0	0	0
Afghan Infrastructure Fd.	0	0	0.4	0.4	0.3	0.2	0	0	0	0	0	0	0	0
Cmdrs. Emerg. Resp. Fd	0.7	1.0	0.3	0.4	0.2	0.0	0	0.7	0.2	0.2	0	0	0	0
Coalition Support	1.4	1.8	2.0	2.1	2.0	1.7	1.7	0.4	0.1	0	0	0.1	0	0
Pakistan Counterinsurgency Fd.	0.4	0.0	0.8	0	0	0	0	0	0	0	0	0	0	0
Task Force for Business Stability Ops	0	0	0	0	0.2	0.1	0	0	0	0	0	0	0	0
Office of Sec. Cooperation- Iraq	0	0	0	0	0	0	0	0	0	0	0	0.5	0.2	0.1
Subtotal: Programmatic Spt.	**8.8**	**12.9**	**17.5**	**16.6**	**9.5**	**7.7**	**6.2**	**4.8**	**2.1**	**2.1**	**0.0**	**0.6**	**0.2**	**0.1**
Other Costs in Billions of $														
Temporary End Strength Army and USMC	0.0	0.0	1.0	1.8	5.8	4.7	2.3	0.0	0.0	0.9	0.1	0.0	0.0	0.0
Unexploded Ordnance	0.0	0.0	0.0	0.0	0.0	0.0	0.0	0.0	0.0	0.0	0.0	0.0	0.0	0.0
Counterterrorism Partnerships Fund (CTPF)	0.0	0.0	0.0	0.0	0.0	0.0	ns	0.0	0.0	0.0	0.0	0.0	0.0	ns

Table D-1. (Continued)

By Category Fiscal Year	Afghan War/OEF							Iraq War/OIF and OND						
	2009	2010	2011	2012	2013	2014	2015	2009	2010	2011	2012	2013	2014	2015
European Reassurance initiative (ERI)	0.0	0.0	0.0	0.0	0.0	0.0	ns	0.0	0.0	0.0	0.0	0.0	0.0	ns
Other/Classified activities[f]	3.3	6.6	7.0	10.5	5.7	3.7	2.7	2.7	5.3	4.1	0.5	1.2	0.0	ns
Subtotal: Other[g]	**3.3**	**6.6**	**8.0**	**12.3**	**11.6**	**8.4**	**5.1**	**2.7**	**5.3**	**5.0**	**0.6**	**1.2**	**0.0**	**0.0**
WAR TOTAL	**50.2**	**100.9**	**114.0**	**106.1**	**86.0**	**70.4**	**49.7**	**89.1**	**61.7**	**45.0**	**9.6**	**3.2**	**0.8**	**0.3**

Sources: Functional table in DOD's OCO Budget overviews for FY2009-FY2015. DOD did not segregate functional categories by operations before FY2009.

Programmatic costs cover a wide range of tools that support troop operations indirectly and so do not necessarily reflect the pace of war operations. The largest amounts for the training of Afghan and Iraq security forces reflect both policy decisions about the size of the Afghan and Iraq armies and police, as well as the U.S. commitment to equipping and training those forces.

Other tools, like coalition support to reimburse primarily Pakistan for its logistical costs of conducting counterterror operations that support the United States, have been funded between $1.0 billion and $2.0 billion over the years. A local tool, the Commanders' Emergency Response Fund (CERP), is intended to help U.S. commanding officers win the support of local populations by providing funds for local development projects, and generally reflects the pace of operations and troop levels. Funds to research and buy new systems to defeat Improvised Explosive Devices or land mines grew as it became clear that this was the weapon of choice for insurgents.

End Notes

[1] White House, "Statement by the President on Afghanistan," May 27, 2014; http://www.whitehouse. gov/ the-press-office/ 2014/05/27/statement-president-afghanistan.

[2] See Table S-10 in OMB, *Fiscal Year 2015, Budget*; http://www.whitehouse.gov/omb/budget/ Overview. "Summary Tables;" March 10, 2014; http://www.whitehouse.gov/sites/default/ files/omb/budget/fy2015/assets/tables.pdf. For amended request, see Office of Management and Budget, "Estimate #2—FY 2015 Budget Amendments: Department of Defense (DOD) and Department of State and Other International Programs (State/OIP) to update the FY 2015 Overseas Contingency Operations funding levels; for both DOD and State/OIP to implement the Counterterrorism Partnerships Fund and the European Reassurance Initiative; and for State/OIP peacekeeping costs in the Central African Republic."June 26, 2014; http://www.whitehouse.gov/sites/default/files/omb/assets/budget_amendments/ final_fy_2015_oco_amendment_-_062414.pdf; OMB, "Fact Sheet: The Administration's Fiscal Year 2015 Overseas Contingency Operations (OCO) Request," June 26, 2014; http://www.whitehouse.gov/the-press-office/2014/06/26/fact-sheet-administration-s-fiscal-year-2015-overseas-contingency-operat.

[3] CBO, "The Continuing Appropriations Resolution, 2015 (H.J.Res. 124), Including the Amendment in Part A of H. Rept. 113- 600," as Approved by the House Committee on Rules on September 15, 2014; http://www.cbo.gov/sites/default/files/ hjres124_0.pdf. The CBO figure includes all funding designated as OCO. The CRS total includes VA Medical war-related funding, which is not designated as OCO.

[4] White House, "Fact Sheet: The Administration's Fiscal Year 2015 Overseas Contingency Operations Request," May 27, 2014; http://www.whitehouse.gov/the-press-office/2014/05/28/fact-sheet-administration-s-fiscal-year-2015-overseas-contingency-operat.; Department of Defense, Fiscal Year 2015, Office of the Under Secretary of Defense/Comptroller, *Counterterrorism Partnerships Fund and the European Reassurance Initiative*, p. 12, June 2014; http://comptroller. defense.gov/Portals/45/Documents/ defbudget/fy2015/amendment/FY2015_OCO_CTPF_and_%20ERI.pdf.

[5] The most well-known example is the book by Linda Bilmes and Joseph Stiglitz, *The Three Trillion Dollar War* (2008). Another well-known example is Eisenhower Study Group, Costs of War project at Brown University, "The Costs of War Since 2001: Iraq, Afghanistan, and Pakistan," Executive Summary, June 2011; see http://costsofwar.org/article/economic-cost-summary.

[6] CBO, Director's Blog, "Comments on Bilmes and Stiglitz, *The Three Trillion Dollar War* (2008);" http://cboblog.cbo.gov/?p=79.

[7] This level matched the Administration's FY2014 request before congressional action.

[8] §1236 in Rules Committee print 113-58, House amendment to the text of S. 1847, http://www.armed-services.senate.gov/imo/media/doc/CPRT-113-HPRT-RU00-S1847.pdf

[9] Sec. 1236 in Ibid. "Appropriate" committees include armed services, appropriations, and international affairs committees of both houses.

[10] Sec. 1236(j) in Ibid.

[11] See Sec. 1236 for Iraq Train and Equip and other sections in Title XII for expansion of current Train and Equip programs rather than the Administration's proposal; Rules Committee print 113-58, House amendment to the text of S. 1847, http://www.armed-services.senate.gov/imo/media/doc/CPRT-113-HPRT-RU00-S1847.pdf.

[12] For State/USAID and VA Medical, these figures include funding in their base budgets, and for DOD funds in both Title IX of DOD's appropriations acts, and funds in supplementals. In the case of DOD, these figures also include funds transferred to war funding from DOD's base budget.

[13] All DOD war spending has been designated as either emergency or OCO. State Department/USAID spending for Afghanistan and Iraq has been appropriated in either the base budget or as emergency or OCO funding.

[14] CRS calculated this figure using DOD-provided data and "Table 2 – Non-War Programs or Programs Whose Execution Is Not Included in the DOD Cost of War Report" in Department of Defense (DoD), *Estimate of Cost of War Report* for each fiscal year and other information from DOD. CRS did include war-related National Intelligence Funding, which is war-related but is not implemented or tracked by DOD. All but two of the 24 bills enacted since 9/11 that provided DOD war funding was designated as either emergency or for OCO based on a CRS review.

[15] This figure does not include the cost of benefits for OEF/OIF/OND veterans, which is not available from the VA.

[16] VA does not distinguish veterans of the first Iraq war in 1991 from those from the Afghan and Iraq wars of the past 13 year in its benefit programs but does in discretionary funding for VA medical care.

[17] For details, see CRS Report RL31339, *Iraq: Post-Saddam Governance and Security*, by Kenneth Katzman. Some 230 U.S. military remain in Iraq as part of the Office of Security Cooperation; that number was expected to have declined to 125 in FY2014; see Department of Defense, Under Secretary of Defense, Comptroller, *Addendum, Overseas Contingency Operation*, May 2013, p. 9 shows military strength of 230 in FY2013 and 125 in FY2014.

[18] See CRS Report RL30588, *Afghanistan: Post-Taliban Governance, Security, and U.S. Policy*, by Kenneth Katzman, and Senate Armed Services Committee, Transcript, "Hearing on Nominations of Admiral Mullen for Reappointment to the Grade of Admiral and Reappointment as chairman of the Joint Chiefs of Staff," September 15, 2009, p. 6. See also the White House, "Remarks by the President in Address to the Nation on the Way Forward in Afghanistan and Pakistan," Delivered at West Point, December 1, 2009; http://www.whitehouse.gov/the-press-office/remarks-president-address-nation-way-forward-afghanistan-and-pakistan.

[19] DOD, "Press Conference with Secretary of Defense Gates," December 14, 2009; http://www.defenselink.mil/transcripts/transcript.aspx?transcriptid=4333. The 21,000 increase was funded in the FY2009 Supplemental and the FY2010 DOD Appropriations Act (Title IX, P.L. 111-118, enacted December 16, 2009).

[20] White House, "Remarks by the President in Address to the Nation on the Way Forward in Afghanistan and Pakistan," Delivered at West Point, December 1, 2009; http://www.whitehouse.gov/the-press-office/remarks-president-address-nation-way-forward-afghanistan-and-pakistan.

[21] White House, "Remarks by the President on the State of the Union," February 12, 2013; http://www.whitehouse.gov/the-press-office/2013/02/12/remarks-president-state-union-address.

[22] White House, "Statement by the President on Afghanistan," May 27, 2014; http://www.whitehouse.gov/the-press-office/2014/05/27/statement-president-afghanistan. Reuters, "Obama to Announce Afghanistan Troop Plans Shortly: Kerry," May 14, 2014; *Foreign Policy*, FP's Situation Report, "Where's the decision on Afghanistan?" May 22, 2013; fp@foreignpolicy.com.; *USA Today*, "White House scaling back military support for Afghan forces," by Jim Michaels, June 4, 2013. About 1,800 of these troops would conduct counter-terror operations.

[23] White House, "U.S.-Afghan Enduring Strategic Partnership Agreement," May 1, 2012; http://www.whitehouse.gov/ sites/default/files/2012.06.01u.s.-afghanistanspasignedtext.pdf. CRS Report RL30588, *Afghanistan: Post-Taliban Governance, Security, and U.S. Policy*, by Kenneth Katzman.

[24] *Defense One*, "Close to a Deal: U.S., Afghans Agree on Single Text," by Gayle Tzemach Lemmon, August 3, 2013; *New York Times*, "Amid Drawdown, Fears of Taliban Resurgence and Economic Collapse," by Matthew Rosenberg, May 29, 2014, Pg. A11. CRS Report RL30588, *Afghanistan: Post-Taliban Governance, Security, and U.S. Policy*, by Kenneth Katzman.

[25] Department of Defense, *Report on Progress Toward Security and Stability in Afghanistan, Sec. 1230 Report*, p. 22, October 2014; http://www.defense.gov/pubs/Oct2014_Report_Final.pdf.

[26] See "Placemat" in International Security Assistance Force, "Facts and Figures," for ISAF troop levels; http://www.nato/ int/isaf/docu/epub/pdf/placement.pdf. For current levels, see CRS Report RL30588, *Afghanistan: Post-Taliban Governance, Security, and U.S. Policy*, by Kenneth Katzman.

[27] This is reflected in a jump from 28,000 in December 2011 for OEF support to 67,000 in January 2012 when the Iraq mission ended. The previous month, OIF in-theater support was shown as 42,900, and OIF in-theater support as 28,000. see DOD, "Boots on the Ground report," December 2011 and January 2012.

[28] DOD's new estimate for ONE is $8 billion rather than the $6.5 billion shown in an earlier DOD briefing. For more information, see CRS Report RL31187, *Combating Terrorism: 2001 Congressional Debate on Emergency Supplemental Allocations*, and CRS Report RL31829, *Supplemental Appropriations FY2003: Iraq Conflict, Afghanistan, Global War on Terrorism, and Homeland Security*, both by Amy Belasco and Larry Nowels.

[29] See for example, Department of State, Congressional Budget Justification, Appendix 1: Department of State Operations, Fiscal Year 2015; http://www.state.gov/documents/organization/223495.pdf.

[30] *Executive Budget Summary Function 150 & Other International Programs*, Fiscal Year 2012, p. 143; http://www.state.gov/documents/organization/183755.pdf. State Department, "Fact Sheet, FY 2012 State and USAID - Overseas Contingency Operations," February 14, 2011; http://www.state.gov/s/d/rm/rls/fs/2011/156555.htm.

[31] CRS, Foreign Affairs Overseas Contingency Operations (OCO): Background and Current Issues, November 19, 2014; http://www.crs.gov/products/if/pdf/IF00063.pdf?Source=search.

[32] Department of State, Foreign Operations, and Related Programs, Budget Amendment Summary, Fiscal Year 2015, 7-2-14, p. vi; http://www.state.gov/documents/organization/228924.pdf.

[33] 38 U.S.C. §1710(e)(1)(D) states that a veteran who served on active duty in a theater of combat operations (as determined by the Secretary of Veterans Affairs, in consultation with the

Secretary of Defense) during a period of war after the Persian Gulf War, or in combat against a hostile force during a period of hostilities after November 11, 1998, is eligible for hospital care, medical services, and nursing home care for any illness, even if there is insufficient medical evidence to conclude that such condition is attributable to such service.

[34] The statutory definition of "off-budget" refers to Social Security and Postal Service revenues and spending; see OMB, *FY2014 Budget, Analytical Perspectives, p. 138*; http://www.whitehouse.gov/sites/default/files/omb/budget/ fy2014/assets/31_1.pdf.

[35] Secretary of Defense Chuck Hagel in House Armed Services Committee, Hearing transcript, "U.S. Strategy on ISIL," September 18, 2014.

[36] CRS Report R41965, *The Budget Control Act of 2011*, by Bill Heniff Jr., Elizabeth Rybicki, and Shannon M. Mahan.

[37] The spending limits set in the Budget Control Act of 2011 (P.L. 112-25) were modified in the Taxpayer Relief Act of 2012 (P.L. 112-240) and the Bipartisan Budget Act of 2013 (P.L. 113-73).

[38] See DOD monthly Cost of War briefing slides, table entitled "Funding Appropriated Through War-Related Requests, FY2001-FY2013," March 2014, and CRS calculation based on tables in Joint Explanatory Statement in *Congressional Record*, January 15, 2013, p. H800 to p.H806.

[39] CRS estimates reflecting DOD's 95% share of BCA caps for national defense (budget function 050) in each budget request.

[40] Department of Defense, "Estimated Impacts of Sequestration-Level Funding: Fiscal Year 2015 Budget Request;" http://www.defense.gov/pubs/2014_Estimated_Impacts_of_Sequestration -Level_Funding_April.pdf.

[41] CRS calculations comparing estimated BCA "sequester" caps with FY2015 Administration DOD plan.

[42] OMB, *Fiscal Year 2015 Budget of the U.S. Government*, p. 11 and p. 30, March 4, 2014; http://www.whitehouse.gov/sites/default/files/omb/budget/fy2015/assets/budget.pdf.

[43] Within DOD appropriations acts, war-designated funding has been included in Title IX. Additional war-related military construction has been included in the Military Construction/VA appropriations acts in the same fashion.

[44] See Sec. 1503 in H.Rept. 113-446, "Howard P. 'Buck' McKeon National Defense Authorization Act for Fiscal Year 2015," on H.R. 4435, May 13, 2014, p. 279.

[45] See Sec. 1524 in H.R. 4435 as passed by the House, 5-22-14; http://www.gpo.gov/fdsys/pkg/BILLS-113hr4435eh/ pdf/BILLS-113hr4435eh.pdf. This language reflects OMB's modified criteria included in a letter from OMB Program Associate Director, Steven Kosiak, to DOD Comptroller Robert Hale; these criteria have been issued as budget guidance to the Department of Defense.

[46] See p. 100 in H.Rept. 113-403, report on H.Con.Res. 96, Concurrent Resolution on the Budget, Fiscal Year," April 6, 2015, http://www.gpo.gov/fdsys/pkg/CRPT-113hrpt403/pdf/CRPT-113hrpt403.pdf.

[47] Transcript, House Budget Committee, "Hearing on President Obama's Funding Request for Overseas Contingency Operations," July 17, 2014.

[48] *Ibid.*

[49] Transcript, House Armed Services Committee, "Hearing on President Obama's Proposed Fiscal 2015 Supplemental Budget Request for Overseas Contingency Operations," July 16, 2014.

[50] *Ibid.*

[51] Ibid.

[52] Ibid.

[53] The Senate point of order is section 314(e) of the Budget Act of 1974. See also, CRS Report R41564, *Emergency Designation: Current Budget Rules and Procedures*, by Bill Heniff Jr.

[54] See footnote 5 in CRS Report R41564, *Emergency Designation: Current Budget Rules and Procedures*, by Bill Heniff Jr. Congress first permitted an OCO designation language in the 2006 budget resolution.

[55] The concern first arose when the Army appeared to be running out of the ability to "cash flow" war costs by using its base budget funds temporarily until Congress passed the FY2004 supplemental; see CRS Memo, "Adequacy of Army's FY2004 Funding for Iraq," by Amy Belasco, May 5, 2014; available from author. Starting that year, Congress began to include some but not necessarily all war funding in Title IX of DOD's regular appropriations. These funds were to act as a "bridge" to cover ongoing war costs in the initial months of the fiscal year. Congress continued, however, to designate these funds as emergency so that they were not subject to budget limits. See discussion in CRS Report 98- 721, *Introduction to the Federal Budget Process*, coordinated by Bill Heniff Jr.

[56] DOD, *Financial Management Regulations*, Chapter 12, Sec. 23, "Contingency Operations," p. 23ff; http://www.dod.mil/comptroller/fmr/12/12_23.pdf.

[57] DOD, *Financial Management Regulations*, Chapter 12, Sec. 23, "Contingency Operations," p. 23ff; http://www.dod.mil/comptroller/fmr/12/12_23.pdf.

[58] See DOD monthly Cost of War briefing slides, table entitled "Funding Appropriated through War-related Requests, FY2001-FY2013," March 2014, and CRS analysis of congressional reports on supplementals and other war funding, and CRS calculation based on tables in Joint Explanatory Statement in *Congressional Record*, January 15, 2013, p. H800 to p.H806.

[59] Under Secretary of Defense, Memorandum for Secretaries of the Military Departments, "Fiscal Year (FY) 2008- 2013 Program and Budget Review," July 19, 2006, p. 34-49, specifically pp. 36, 39, 41.

[60] Deputy Secretary of Defense Gordon England, Memorandum for Secretaries of the Military Departments, "Ground Rules and Process for FY'07 Spring Supplemental," October 25, 2006.

[61] See Chapter III, p. 19ff in White House, "National Security Strategy," May 2010; https://digitalndulibrary.ndu.edu/ cdm4/document.php?CISOROOT=/strategy&CISOPTR=8929&REC=1; See Chapter III in White House, "The National Security Strategy of the United States of America," March 2006; https://digitalndulibrary.ndu.edu/cdm4/document.php?CISOROOT=/strategy&CISOPTR=5286&REC=2.

[62] CRS calculation based on Table 2-1 Department of Defense, Office of the Under Secretary of Defense (Comptroller), *National Defense Budget Estimates for FY 2015*, April 2014; http://comptroller.defense.gov/Portals/45/Documents/defbudget/fy2015/FY15_Green_Book.pdf.

[63] CBO, *Replacing and Repairing Equipment Used In Iraq and Afghanistan: The Army's Reset Program* by Frances M. Lussier, September 2007, p. ix, pp. 35-37; available at http://www.cbo.gov/showdoc.cfm?index=8629&sequcence=0& from=7.

[64] Stimson Center, Russell Rumbaugh, *What We Bought: Defense Procurement from FY01 to FY10*, p. 9, October 28, 2011; http://www.stimson.org/books-reports/what-we-bought-defense-procurement-from-fy01-to-fy10/

[65] *Ibid.*

[66] OMB, "Criteria for War/Overseas Contingency Operations Funding Requests," February 26, 2009, revised 2010.

[67] CRS Report R40567, *Defense: FY2010 Authorization and Appropriations*, coordinated by Pat Towell.

[68] CBO estimated that the Army's modularity initiative would only make available an additional 6,000 to 7,000 troops. The RAND study argued that the types of units created were not those most needed. RAND, *Stretched Thin: Army Forces for Sustained Operations*, 7-15-05; http://www.rand.org/pubs/monographs/2005/RAND_MG362.pdf. CBO, *An Analysis of*

the Military's Ability to Sustain an Occupation in Iraq: an Update, October 5, 2005; http://www.cbo.gov/ ftpdocs/66xx/doc6682/10-05-05-IraqLetter.pdf.

69 Secretary of the Army, "Sec. 323 report required by the FY2007 National Defense Authorization Act, P.L. 109-364," February 14, 2007, p. 4.

70 Program Budget Decision 753, "Other Secretary of Defense Decisions," December 23, 2004, p. 1.

71 Ibid., and CRS Report RL32476, *U.S. Army's Modular Redesign: Issues for Congress*, by Andrew Feickert. CBO estimated that adding two divisions to the Army—roughly equivalent to the President's proposal—would require an additional $108 billion between FY2008 and FY2017. CBO, *Budget Options*, February 2007, pp. 9-10, http://www.cbo.gov/ftpdocs/78xx/doc7821/02-23-BudgetOptions.pdf.

72 DOD, *FY2008 Global War on Terror Amendment*, October 2007, http://www.defenselink.mil/ comptroller/defbudget/fy2008/Supplemental/FY2008_October_Global_War_On_Terror_Amendment.pdf, pp. 48 and 49.

73 CRS Report RS21754, *Military Forces: What Is the Appropriate Size for the United States?*, by Andrew Feickert. See also DOD, "President Bush's FY 2008 Defense Budget Submission," February 5, 2007, which notes that $12.1 billion was included in the FY2008 request for these increases and $1.6 billion in the FY2008 Global War on Terror requests.

74 Department of Defense, "Sustaining U.S. Global Leadership: Priorities for the 21st Century," p. 6, January 2012; http://www.defense.gov/news/Defense_Strategic_Guidance.pdf. 75 White House, "Remarks by the President at the National Defense University," Washington, DC, May 23, 2013; White House, http://www.whitehouse.gov/the-press-office/2013/05/23/ remarks-president-national-defense-university. See also, Table 4 in Department of Defense, Fiscal Year 2015 Budget Amendment, Overview, Overseas Contingency Operations, June 2014; http://comptroller.defense.gov/Portals/45/Documents/defbudget/fy2015/amendment/ FY2015_Budget_Request_Overview_Book_Amended.pdf. Until these lower personnel levels were achieved, DOD requested and received OCO funding to pay for 49,700 Army and 15,200 Marine Corps personnel active-duty strength that are "over strength" or "above the projected end state needed by these Services [in 2017] to support the new defense strategy." See Department of Defense, Office of the Under Secretary of Defense (Comptroller)/Chief Financial Officer, Fiscal Year 2013 Overview, February 2012, pp. 6-7; http://comptroller.defense.gov/defbudget/fy2013/ FY2013_Budget_Request_Overview_Book.pdf. DOD's policy called for these decreases to occur gradually over several years, primarily through attrition rather than involuntary separations, also a policy choice.

76 For total through FY2008, see Center for Strategic and Budgetary Assessments, Steve Kosiak, *Cost of Wars in Iraq and Afghanistan and Other Military Operations*, 12-15-08; http://www.csbaonline.org/4Publications/PubLibrary/R.20081215.Cost_of_the_Wars_i/R.20081215.Cost_of_the_Wars_i.pdf; for FY2009, see Table 5-11 in DOD, *Fiscal Year 2010: Summary Justification*, May 2009; http://www.defenselink.mil/comptroller/ defbudget/fy2010/fy2010_SSJ.pdf; for FY2010 and FY2011, see Table 8-5 in DOD, *FY2011 Budget Request: Overview*, February 1, 2010; http://comptroller.defense.gov/ defbudget/fy2011/ FY2011_Budget_Request_Overview_Book.pdf. For definition, see Office of the Secretary of Defense, Report to Congress, *Ground Force Equipment Repair, Replacement, and Recapitalization Requirements Resulting from Sustained Combat Operations*, April 2005, p. 8; see also GAO-06-604T, *Defense Logistics: Preliminary Observations on Equipment Reset Challenges and Issues for the Army and Marine Corps*, p. 3. DOD, *FY2008 Global War on Terror Request*, February 2007, Table 3; http://www.dod.mil/comptroller/defbudget/fy2008/fy2007_supplemental/FY2008_Global_War_On_Terror_Request.pdf hereinafter, DOD, *FY2008 GWOT Request.*

77 CRS, Statement of Amy Belasco before the House Budget Committee, "The Growing Cost of the Iraq War," October 24, 2007 http://budget.house.gov/hearings/2007/10.24Belasco _testimony.pdf.

[78] CBO Testimony by Douglas Holtz-Eakin, Director, "The Potential Costs Resulting from Increased Usage of Military Equipment in Ongoing Operations," before the Subcommittee on Readiness, House Armed Services Committee, April 6, 2005, p. 2.

[79] Statement of Peter J. Schoomaker, Chief of Staff, Department of the Army, before the House Armed Services Committee, "Reset Strategies for Ground Equipment and Rotor Craft," June 27, 2006, p.2; see also testimony of Brigadier General Charles Anderson, U.S. Army, House Armed Services Subcommittee on Readiness and Subcommittee on Air and Land Forces Hold, transcript, "Joint Hearing on Costs and Problems of Maintaining Military Equipment in Iraq," January 31, 2007, p. 6.

[80] Testimony of OMB Director Robert Portman before the House Budget Committee, *Hearing on the FY2008 DOD Budget*, February 6, 2007, p. 41 of transcript.

[81] See table inserted by Senator Stevens in *Congressional Record*, August 2, 2006, p. S8571 showing $23.7 billion for reset, including $14 billion in procurement; total funded also provided $4.9 billion for unfunded FY2006 requirement; see also DOD's *Report to Congress, Long-Term Equipment Repair Costs*, September 2006.

[82] Testimony of General Michael Hagee, Marine Corps Commandant before the House Armed Services Committee, "Army and Marine Corps Reset Strategies for Ground Equipment and Rotor Craft," June 27, 2006, p. 41. GAO-07- 439T, Testimony of William Solis before the Subcommittee on Readiness and Air and Land Forces, House Armed Services Committee, January 31, 2007, pp. 2 and 3. In a September 2006 report to Congress, for example, annual reset requirements in FY2008 were estimated to be $13 billion for the Army and about $1 billion for the Marine Corps; see Office of the Secretary of Defense, Report to the Congress, "Long-Term Equipment Repair Costs," September 2006, pp. 24 and 25. Months earlier, in the spring of 2006, the Army estimated that reset requirements would decrease from $13 billion a year to $10.5 billion a year for the next two years and then decline to $2 billion a year if troops were withdrawn over a two-year period; see Army Briefing, "Army Equipment Reset Update," May 18, 2006, p. 8.

[83] CRS, Statement of Amy Belasco before the House Budget Committee, "The Rising Cost of the Iraq War," October 24, 2007; http://budget.house.gov/hearings/2007/10.24Belasco_testimony.pdf.

[84] CRS calculations based on DOD, "Cost of War Execution Report," April 30, 2010.

[85] See for example, Sec. 314 and Sec. 315 and Scc. P.L. 110-32 in the FY2009 Supplemental Appropriations Act applying to "this or any other act," and Sec. 1237 and Sec. 2806, P.L. 111-84, the FY2010 National Defense Authorization Act; see also section, "More Spending for Bases in Afghanistan Raises Questions of Permanency and Execution," in CRS Report R41232, *FY2010 Supplemental for Wars, Disaster Assistance, Haiti Relief, and Other Programs*, coordinated by Amy Belasco. These prohibitions were repeated in annual DOD appropriation and authorization acts.

[86] See for example, Department of Defense, Report on Progress Toward Security and Stability in Afghanistan, Sec. 1230 Report, October 2014, Department of Defense, Report on Progress Toward Security and Stability in Afghanistan; p. 5-p. 6, October 2014; http://www.defense.gov/pubs/Oct2014_Report_Final.pdf.

[87] DOD data provided to CRS for FY2001-FY2008 and tables included in DOD's monthly cost of war reports for September 2009 to June 2014.

[88] White House, Office of the Press Secretary, "Remarks by the President in the State of the Uolsternion Address," February 12, 2013; http://www.whitehouse.gov/the-press-office/2013/02/12/remarks-president-state-union-address.

[89] White House, "Statement by the President on Afghanistan," May 27, 2014; http://www.whitehouse.gov/the-pressoffice/ 2014/05/27/statement-president-afghanistan; White House, Press Release, "Fact Sheet: Bringing the U.S. War in Afghanistan to a Responsible End," May 27,2014.

[90] *Washington Post*, "U.S. plans extra troops for Afghanistan," by Missy Ryan, December 5, 2014.

[91] *Washington Post*, "Afghan mission for U.S. to continue under new authorities," by Karen DeYoung and Missy Ryan; http://www.washingtonpost.com/world/national-security/white-house-gives-commanders-broader-authority-to-supportafghan- troops/2014/11/22/8741f2fc-724e-11e4-ad12-3734c461eab6_story.html.

[92] CRS calculations based on Figure 1 and Table 1 in Department of Defense, Fiscal Year 2015 Budget Amendment, Overview, Overseas Contingency Operations, June 2014; http://comptroller.defense.gov/Portals/45/Documents/ defbudget/fy2015/amendment/FY2015_Budget_Request_Overview_Book_Amended.pdf.

[93] Testimony of DOD Comptroller, Mike McCord before the House Armed Services Committee, Transcript, "Hearing on President Obama's Proposed Fiscal 2015 Supplemental Budget Request for Overseas Contingency Operations," July 16, 2014.

[94] Department of Defense, Under Secretary of Defense, Comptroller, *Addendum, Overseas Contingency Operation*, May 2013, p.1.

[95] Testimony of Robert Work before House Budget Committee, Transcript, "Hearing on President Obama's Funding Request for Overseas Contingency Operations," July 17, 2014–Final.

[96] Department of Defense, *Fiscal Year 2015 Budget Amendment, Overview, Overseas Contingency Operations*, June 2014; p. 2, http://comptroller.defense.gov/Portals/45/ Documents/defbudget/fy2015/amendment/FY2015_Budget_Request_Overview_Book_Am ended.pdf.

[97] Monies can be obligated or de-obligated after their lives expire to adjust already-signed contracts for up to five years, though the adjustments are generally minor.

[98] Statutory language in appropriation acts set the availability or "life" of funds in each account.

[99] Congress sets caps each year in DOD appropriations acts on the overall amount that can be transferred from base budget accounts and separately for Title IX war-designated accounts. See for example, Sec. 8005 in P.L. 113-76, FY2014 Consolidated Appropriations Act; "SEC. 8005. Upon determination by the Secretary of Defense that such (continued...) (...continued) action is necessary in the national interest, he may, with the approval of the Office of Management and Budget, *transfer not to exceed $5,000,000,000 of working capital funds of the Department of Defense or funds made available in this Act* to the Department of Defense for military functions (except military construction) between such appropriations or funds or any subdivision thereof, to be merged with and to be available for the same purposes, and for the same time period, as the appropriation or fund to which transferred." See also vol. 12, chap. 23 in Department of Defense, *Financial Management Regulations*, Contingency Operations; http://www.defenselink.mil/comptroller/fmr/12/ 12_23.pdf.

[100] CRS analysis of data in DOD's cost of war execution reports and its cumulative database as of June 2014.

[101] DOD, Comptroller, "Overseas Contingency Operations (OCO) Request, Various Appropriations, FY14-13 PA," September 8, 2014 (ISIL campaign); http://comptroller.defense.gov/Portals/45/Documents/ execution/reprogramming/fy2014/prior1415s/14-13_PA_OCO_Request.pdf.

[102] DOD, Comptroller, August 2014, Various Appropriations, Ebola, 9-8-14; Ebola FY14-14 PA, http://comptroller.defense.gov/Portals/45/Documents/execution/reprogramming/fy2014/prio r1415s/14- 14_PA_August_2014_Request.pdf. DOD, Comptroller, "Additional Ebola Response," Overseas Humanitarian, Disaster Assistance, 14/15 and Operation and Maintenance, Army, 14/14, 9-5-14; $500 million, Ebola, deemed OCO; http://comptroller. defense.gov/Portals/45/Documents/execution/reprogramming/fy2014/prior1415s/14-17_PA_Ebola_Response.pdf. Although the three reprogrammings totaled $1.0 billion, the four Congressional defense committees capped the total at $750 million.

[103] DOD, Comptroller, "Overseas Contingency Operations (OCO) Request, Various Appropriations, FY14-13 PA," September 8, 2014 (ISIL campaign); http://comptroller.defense.gov/Portals/45/Documents/execution/reprogramming/ fy2014/prior1415s/14-13_PA_OCO_Request.pdf. Congress ultimately placed a $750

million cap on DOD's Ebola humanitarian assistance. These factors would presumably also reduce costs anticipated in FY2015.

[104] See Appendix B, OMB, "Revised War Funding Criteria," September 2010.

[105] The BCA (P.L. 112-25) required a sequester in FY2013.

[106] Memorandum, Deputy Secretary of Defense, Ashton Carter to the services and defense agencies, "Planning for Uncertainty," January 10, 2013.

[107] Memorandum, Secretary of Defense, Chuck Hagel to the Services and defense agencies, "Furloughs," May 14, 2013.

[108] CRS calculations based on table provided by DOD tracking individual accounts from BA enacted to post-sequester funding levels, September 2013.

[109] Department of Defense, Office of the Under Secretary of Defense (Comptroller)/Chief Financial Officer, *Overview, Overseas Contingency Operations*, p. 2-p.3, June 2014; http://comptroller.defense.gov/Portals/45/Documents/ defbudget/fy2015/amendment/FY2015_Budget_Request_Overview_Book_Amended.pdf. See also, Testimony of Michael McCord, Under Secretary of Defense, Comptroller before House Armed Services Committee, *Hearing on President Obama's Proposed Fiscal 2015 Supplemental Budget Request for Overseas Contingency Operations*, June 16, 2014, pp. 3-4, July 16, 2014.

[110] With fewer troops, the services will not need to rely on as many reservists, with the additional activation costs.

[111] See CRS, Statement of Amy Belasco before the House Budget Committee, Hearing on "The Rising Cost of the Iraq War," October 24, 2007; http://budget.house.gov/hearings/ 2007/10.24Belasco_testimony.pdf; Commission on Wartime Contracting in Iraq and Afghanistan, "At What Cost: Contingency Contracting in Iraq and Afghanistan," Interim Report, pp.34, June 2009; http://www.wartimecontracting.gov/docs/CWC_Interim_Report _At_What_Cost_06-10- 09.pdf. Commission on wartime Contracting, Final Report, 8-31-11; http://www.sigar.mil/.

[112] See Congressional Record, Joint Explanatory Statement for H.R. 933, "Department of Defense, Military Construction and Veterans Affairs, and Full-Year Continuing Appropriations Act, 2013,'' p. 998 and p. 1240. See also troop reduction cut of $380.1 million shown on p. 794 in H.Rept. 112-331. See also congressional action in P.L. 113- 118 (H.Rept. 111-118) to transfer $5.0 billion from DOD military personnel and O&M accounts to the Overseas Contingency Operations Transfer Fund (OCOTF) because "The nature of military action in Operations Enduring Freedom and Iraqi Freedom is expected to change significantly in fiscal year 2010. Therefore, the Services cannot accurately budget for these operations. The OCOTF account provides flexibility to transfer funds to the needed appropriation account once costs are known." (H.Rept. 111-230, p. 424)

[113] Operational costs include war funds for military personnel and O&M excluding programs like coalition support and training of Afghan and Iraq security forces; investment funds include war-designated procurement, RDT&E, and military construction.

[114] CRS calculations, based on figures shown in **Figure 7**.

[115] Department of Defense, Fiscal Year 2015, Office of the Under Secretary of Defense/Comptroller, "Counterterrorism Partnerships Fund and the European Reassurance Initiative," June 2014, pp. 1-2; http://comptroller.defense.gov/Portals/ 45/Documents/ defbudget/fy2015/amendment/FY2015_OCO_CTPF_and_%20ERI.pdf.

[116] Office of Management and Budget, Estimate #2—FY 2015 Budget Amendments: Department of Defense (DOD) and Department of State and Other International Programs (State/OIP) to update the FY 2015 Overseas Contingency Operations funding levels; for both DOD and State/OIP to implement the Counterterrorism Partnerships Fund and the European Reassurance Initiative; and for State/OIP peacekeeping costs in the Central African Republic.—06/26/2014, pp. 26-30; http://www.whitehouse.gov/sites/default/files/omb/ assets/budget_amendments/ final_fy_2015_oco_amendment_-_062414.pdf.

[117] Ibid., p. 12-p. 27.

[118] Congress appropriated $20 billion in the government-wide Emergency Response Fund which could be spent by the President at his discretion (P.L. 107-38). In the FY2002 DOD conference report, DOD also received another $3.5 billion in the newly established Defense Emergency Response Fund (DERF) subject to allocations in H.Rept. 107-350 (p. 423).

[119] Congress appropriated $20 billion in the government-wide Emergency Response Fund which could be spent by the President at his discretion (P.L. 107-38). DOD also received another $3.5 billion in the DERF but had to follow allocations that were set in the FY2002 DOD Conference report (H.Rept. 107-350, p. 423).

[120] H.Rept. 107-593, p.17 and 128.

[121] Congress rescinded $3.5 billion of the $15.6 billion originally appropriated to the IFF and included ceilings for certain purposes, such as intelligence, within the total.

[122] CRS Report RL32422, *The Administration's FY2005 Request for $25 Billion for Operations in Iraq and Afghanistan: Precedents, Options, and Congressional Action*, by Amy Belasco and Stephen Daggett.

[123] For President's West Point speech, see White House, Office of the Press Secretary, "Remarks by the President at the United States Military Academy Commencement Ceremony," U.S. Military Academy-West Point, West Point, New York, May 28, 2014; http://www.whitehouse.gov/the-press-office/2014/05/28/remarks-president-west-point-academy-commencementceremony.

[124] Department of Defense, Fiscal Year 2015, Office of the Under Secretary of Defense/ Comptroller, "Counterterrorism Partnerships Fund and the European Reassurance Initiative," June 2014, pp. 1-p. 11, http://comptroller. defense.gov/Portals/45/ Documents/ defbudget/fy2015/amendment/FY2015_OCO_CTPF_and_%20ERI.pdf.

[125] Some of these funds are financed in the base budget and some in OCO. House Budget Committee, Transcript, "Hearing on President Obama's Funding Request for Overseas Contingency Operations," July 17, 2014; House Armed Services Committee, Transcript, "Hearing on President Obama's Proposed Fiscal 2015 Supplemental Budget Request for Overseas Contingency Operations," July 16, 2014.

[126] House Armed Services Committee, transcript, "Hearing on President Obama's Proposed Fiscal 2015 Supplemental Budget Request for Overseas Contingency Operations," July 16, 2014.

[127] Sec. 149 (f) and Sec.101(a)(3) of the Continuing Appropriations Resolution, 2015, P.L. 113-164.

[128] CRS Report R43727, *Proposed Train and Equip Authorities for Syria: In Brief*, by Christopher M. Blanchard and Amy Belasco.

[129] Ibid.

[130] This practice is known as "cashflowing," where DOD finances military operations with current funds that were to be used for other purposes, in anticipation that Congress will later provide appropriations.

[131] CRS Report R43760, *A New Authorization for Use of Military Force Against the Islamic State: Comparison of Current Proposals in Brief*, by Matthew C. Weed.

[132] For a full discussion of the budgetary and political-military issues, see CRS Report R43727, *Proposed Train and Equip Authorities for Syria: In Brief*, by Christopher M. Blanchard and Amy Belasco.

[133] Senate Armed Services Committee, "Fact Sheet: Highlights of the NDAA," p. 6, December 4, 2014, http://armedservices.house.gov/index.cfm/files/serve?File_id=F477F464-90AE-4B7A-AD7A-438065807D04.

[134] This authority is currently available under 10 U.S.C. Section 127d; see also in Department of Defense, Fiscal Year 2015, Office of the Under Secretary of Defense/Comptroller, "Counterterrorism Partnerships Fund and the European Reassurance Initiative," June 2014, p. 5, http://comptroller.defense.gov/Portals/45/Documents/defbudget/fy2015/amendment/FY2015_OCO_CTPF_and_%20ERI.pdf .

[135] The cap is set by statute within the Defensewide O&M account. See also CRS Report R41832, *Pakistan-U.S. Relations*, by K. Alan Kronstadt. Smaller amounts were provided to

neighboring countries neighboring Afghanistan who participate in the "global war on terror."

[136] Counter-insurgency funding was also provided to Pakistan in the State Department's Pakistan Counterinsurgency Capability Fund; see CRS Report R42116, *Pakistan: U.S. Foreign Aid Conditions, Restrictions, and Reporting Requirements*, by Susan B. Epstein and K. Alan Kronstadt.

[137] CRS Report R42094, *The Lord's Resistance Army: The U.S. Response*, by Alexis Arieff and Lauren Ploch Blanchard.

[138] CRS Report RS22871, *Department of Defense "Section 1207" Security and Stabilization Assistance: Background and Congressional Concerns, FY2006-FY2010*, by Nina M. Serafino.

[139] CRS Report R42541, *United Nations Convention on the Law of the Sea (UNCLOS): CRS Experts*, by Curry L. Hagerty.

[140] See 10 U.S.C. Section 127d, and DOD; email response to CRS query, November 15, 2014.

[141] CRS comparison of Administration request with enacted version.

[142] CRS excluded coalition support because this authority is reimbursement for current logistical support to U.S. operations rather than a partnership to expand capacity through train-and-equip programs.

[143] Department of State, Foreign Operations, and Related Programs, "Budget Amendment Summary, Fiscal Year 2015, http://www.state.gov/documents/organization/228924.pdf. The Administration request would required "concurrence" by the Secretary of State whereas H.J.Res. 124 requires "coordination"; see Table 1 in CRS Report R43727, *Proposed Train and Equip Authorities for Syria: In Brief*, by Christopher M. Blanchard and Amy Belasco.

[144] RAND, "Review of Security Cooperation Mechanisms Combatant Commands Utilize to Build Partner Capacity," by Jennifer D. P. Moroney, David E. Thaler, Joe Hogler, 2013, prepared for the Joint Staff and OSD/CAPE, p. xv, p. xvi; http://www.rand.org/content/dam/rand/pubs/research_reports/RR400/RR413/RAND_RR413.sum.pdf.

[145] Ibid., p. xix, p. xxi, and p. xxii.

[146] Ibid., p. xiii, and throughout.

[147] RAND, "How Successful Are U.S. Efforts to Build Capacity in Developing Countries? A Framework to Assess the Global Train and Equip '1206' Programs," by Jennifer D. P. Moroney, Beth Grill, Joe Hogler, Lianne Kennedy-Bouldali, Christorpher Paul, pp. xiii, 4, 2013; http://www.rand.org/content/dam/rand/pubs/research_reports/RR400/RR413/RAND_RR413.pdf.

[148] CRS Report RS22855, *Security Assistance Reform: "Section 1206" Background and Issues for Congress* , by Nina M. Serafino, pp. 14, 18.

[149] RAND, "What Works Best When Building Partner Capacity and Under What Circumstances?" by Christopher Paul, Colin P. Clarke, Beth Grill, Stephanie Young, Jennifer D. P. Moroney, Joe Hogler, and Christine Leah, pp. xvii-xx, 2013, http://www.rand.org/content/dam/rand/pubs/monographs/MG1200/MG1253z1/RAND_MG1253z1.pdf.

[150] RAND, "Security Cooperation Amidst Political Uncertainty: An Agenda for Future Research," by Larry Hanauer and Stephanie Pezard, " July 2014 http://www.rand.org/content/dam/rand/pubs/working_papers/WR1000/WR1052/ RAND_WR1052.pdf.

[151] David Remnick, "Going the Distance, On and Off the Road with Barack Obama," Annals of the Presidency, *The New Yorker*,, January 27, 2014, http://www.newyorker.com/magazine/2014/01/27/going-the-distance-2.

[152] Office of the Secretary of Defense, Department of Defense Budget, Fiscal Year (FY) 2015, "Justification for FY 2015 Overseas Contingency Operations (OCO), Afghanistan Security Forces Fund (ASFF)," June 2014; http://comptroller.defense.gov/Portals/45/Documents/defbudget/fy2015/FY2015_ASFF_Justification_Book-Final.pdf.

[153] During execution, the funds are transferred to Army O&M, which implements the programs. Based on a statutory requirement, Congress receives semi-annual reports on progress in meeting such security needs.

[154] A GAO report suggested that there would be an Iraqi budget surplus of from $67 billion to $79 billion in 2008 due to oil prices; Members called for "burdensharing" by Iraq in the rebuilding of its security forces. GAO-08-1144T, Statement of Joseph A. Christoff before the House Budget Committee, "Stabilizing and Rebuilding Iraq: Iraqi Revenues, Expenditures, and Surplus," p. 3, September 16, 2008.

[155] See Explanatory Statement for H.R. 2642 in *Congressional Record*, May 19, 2008, p. S4337; and Sec. 1508 in S. 3001, the FY2009 National Defense Authorization Act. Sec. 9205, P.L. 110-252.

[156] See Section 1321, P.L. 110-181 Report, "United States Plan for Sustaining the Afghanistan National Security Forces," April 2010.

[157] CRS Report R41232, *FY2010 Supplemental for Wars, Disaster Assistance, Haiti Relief, and Other Programs*, coordinated by Amy Belasco; and Special Inspector General for Afghanistan Reconstruction, "Actions Needed to Improve the Reliability of Afghan Security Force Assessments," June 29, 2010, http://www.sigar.mil/pdf/audits/SIGAR%20Audit-10-11.pdf.

[158] The reporting ended as the U.S. presence diminished making it difficult to assess conditions. This reporting requirement was first required in H.Rept. 109-72 accompanying H.R. 1268, Emergency Supplemental Appropriations Act for Defense, the Global War on Terror, and Tsunami Relief, 2005, P.L. 109-13. For the final report, see Department of Defense, *Measuring Stability and Security in Iraq*, June 2010, Report to Congress In accordance with the Department of Defense Supplemental Appropriations Act 2008 (Section 9204, P.L. 110-252), http://www.defense.gov/pubs/pdfs/June_9204_Sec_Def_signed_20_Aug_2010.pdf.

[159] "Investigation Finds 50,000 'Ghost' Soldiers in Iraqi Army, Prime Minister Says," Washington Post, http://www.washingtonpost.com/world/middle_east/investigation-finds-50000-ghost-soldiers-in-iraqi-army-prime-minister-says/ 2014/11/30/d8864d6c-78ab-11e4-9721-80b3d95a28a9_story.html.

[160] DOD, *Section 9204 Report, Measuring Security and Stability in Iraq*, pp. vi-ix, June 2010, http://www.defense.gov/pubs/pdfs/ June_9204_Sec_Def_signed_20_Aug_2010.pdf.

[161] Ibid., pp. 28- 37; quote from p. x.

[162] Statement of Secretary of Defense Leon Panetta before the Senate Armed Services Committee in hearing on "Security Issues Relating to Iraq,"112th Congress, First Session, November 15, 2011, p. 8.

[163] Ibid., p. 174.

[164] Ibid., pp. 178-179 and 191ff.

[165] Special Inspector General for Iraq Reconstruction, Quarterly Report to the United States Congress, SIGIR Observations, p. 10, April 30, 2013, http://cybercemetery.unt.edu/archive/sigir/20131001091934/http://www.sigir.mil/files/quarterlyreports/April2013/Report_-_April_2013.pdf.

[166] Anthony H. Cordesman, Sam Khazai, and Daniel Dewit, "Shaping Iraq's Security Forces, US-Iranian Competition Series," Center for Strategic and International Affairs, pp. 10-12, December 16, 2013, http://csis.org/files/publication/ 131213_Iraq_Security_Forces.pdf.

[167] John McCain, "Senators Send Letter to President Obama on Iraq as PM Maliki Visits DC," press release from the Office of Senator John McCain, October 29, 2013, http://www.mccain.senate.gov/public/index.cfm/pressreleases? ID=81e7d512-8a62- 4a63-a573-bf81867b9598.

[168] Loveday Morris, "Iraqi Army Struggles in Battle Against Islamist Fighters in Anbar Province," *Washington Post*, , http://www.washingtonpost.com/world/middle_east/iraqi-army-struggles-in-battle-against-islamist-fighters-in-anbar-province/ 2014/02/25/b76792d2-9b00-11e3-8112-52fdf646027b_story.html.

[169] Loveday Morris, "Iraqi Army Faces Death and Desertions as It Struggles with Anbar Offensive," *Washington Post*, May 8, 2014; 2014, http://www.washingtonpost.com/world/middle_east/iraqi-army-faces-death-and-desertions-as-it-struggles-withanbar-offensive/2014/05/08/83720f79-6cd2-4c7c-883b-dfe181ce7a5b_story.html.

[170] For the latest quarterly report, see Department of Defense, *Report on Progress Toward Security and Stability in Afghanistan*, Sec. 1230 report, April 2014, http://www.defense.gov/pubs/April_1230_Report_Final.pdf.

[171] Ibid., pp.31-32, 43, and 54.

[172] Ibid., pp. 31-35, 45.

[173] Ibid., pp. 41-43, 52-54.

[174] Executive Summary in Center for Naval Analysis, "Independent Assessment of the Afghan National Security Forces," by Jonathan Schroden et. al., January 2014, http://www.cna.org/sites/default/files/research/CNA%20Independent%20Assessment%20of%20the%20ANSF.pdf.

[175] Special Inspector General for Afghanistan Reconstruction, Letter to Kerry, Hagel, Shah about oversight concerns, Special Project 14-14, October 10, 2013, http://www.sigar.mil/pdf/alerts/SIGAR_14-4-SP.pdf.

[176] Sec. 1110 in P.L. 108-106, FY2004 Emergency Supplemental Appropriations Act for Defense and for the Reconstruction of Iraq and Afghanistan," November 6, 2003.

[177] For more information about these reconstruction programs, see CRS Report R40699, *Afghanistan: U.S. Foreign Assistance*, by Curt Tarnoff.

[178] Office of the Under Secretary of Defense (Comptroller)/CFO, Department of Defense, "Budget Execution: Processes and Flexibility," May 2012; "Budget Execution Tutorial," http://comptroller.defense.gov/BudgetExecution.aspx.

[179] For example, caps on war funding were $4 billion (4.7%) of $85 billion in FY2014, $3.5 billion (4.1%) out of $86 billion in FY2013; $4 billion (3.5%) out of $114 billion in FY2012; $3.5 billion (2.5%) out of $114 billion in FY2011; and $4 billion (3.1%) out of $128 billion in FY2010.

[180] DOD obligations for FY2014 have been slower than in the previous five years, suggesting that substantial one-year monies may lapse. In addition, DOD requested reprogrammings using $2.6 billion O&M, Army as a source because the withdrawals have been faster than anticipated. If less funds are needed in FY2014, and the withdrawal is ahead of schedule, the FY2015 request may also be over-stated.

[181] DOD, "Special Report, Operation Inherent Resolve, Targeted Operations Against ISIL Terrorists," December 8, 2014 , http://www.defense.gov/home/features/2014/0814_iraq/.

[182] DOD, Office of the Under Secretary of Defense (Comptroller) *Fiscal Year (FY) 2015 Overseas Contingency Operations (OCO) Budget Amendment Update*, pp. 2-3, November 2014, http://comptroller.defense.gov/Portals/45/Documents/defbudget/ fy2015/amendment/FY15_OCO_Budget_Amendment_Update.pdf.

[183] Office of Management and Budget, Estimate #5—FY 2015 Budget Amendments: Department of Defense (DOD) and Department of State and Other International Programs (State/OIP) to implement the Administration's Strategy to Counter the Islamic State of Iraq and the Levant (ISIL) and update the FY 2015 Overseas Contingency Operations funding levels for both DOD and State/OIP, p. 11, November 10, 2014, http://www.whitehouse.gov/sites/default/files/omb/assets/budget_amendments/ amendment_11_10_14.pdf.

[184] Ibid., p. 12.

[185] Ibid., p. 12.

[186] Sec. 1236 in Rules Committee print 113-58, House amendment to the text of S. 1847, http://www.armed-services.senate.gov/ imo/me.

[187] Ibid., p. 9.

[188] Contributed by Jeremiah Gertler, Foreign Affairs, Defense and Trade Division, CRS.

[189] White House, "Statement by the President on Afghanistan," May 27, 2014, http://www.whitehouse.gov/the-press-office/2014/ 05/27/statement-president-afghanistan;

CRS Report RL30588, *Afghanistan: Post-Taliban Governance, Security, and U.S. Policy*, by Kenneth Katzman.

[190] "U.S. Plans Extra Troops for Afghanistan," *Washington Post*, December 4, 2014. 191 White House, "Fact Sheet: Wales Summit—NATO's Changing Role in Afghanistan," http://www.whitehouse.gov/the-pressoffice/ 2014/09/04/fact-sheet-wales-summit-nato-s-changing-role-afghanistan.

[191] White House, "Fact Sheet: Wales Summit—NATO's Changing Role in Afghanistan," http://www.whitehouse.gov/the-pressoffice/2014/09/04/fact-sheet-wales-summit-nato-s-changing-role-afghanistan.

[192] Declan Walsh and Azam Ahmed, "Mending Alliance, U.S. and Afghanistan Sign Long-Term Security Agreement," *New York Times*, September 30, 2014, http://www.nytimes.com/ 2014/10/01/world/asia/afghanistan-and-us-sign-bilateral-securityagreement. html.

[193] "July deadline missed: DOD Planning To Release OCO Budget 'Migration Guidance' This Fall, *Inside the Pentagon*, August 14, 2014, http://insidedefense.com/Inside-the-Pentagon/ Inside-the-Pentagon-08/14/2014/dod-planning-to-release-oco-budgetmigration- guidance-this-fall/menu-id-148.html.

[194] Jen Judson, "Lawmakers Brace for Long-Term OCO Account," *Politico Pro*, Defense, October 24, 2014.

[195] "Comptroller: Pentagon Discussing Future Of OCO Budget, Increased Spending in Europe," *Inside Defense*, October 2014.

[196] The Administration requested $28 billion in a separate Opportunity, Growth, and Security Initiative that would have breached BCA caps, but the appropriators marked to BCA caps.

[197] Department of Defense, *Report on Progress Toward Security and Stability in Afghanistan*, pp. 1-2, October 2014, http://www.defense.gov/pubs/Oct2014_Report_Final.pdf.

[198] Ibid., p. 15.

[199] International Crisis Group, *Afghanistan's Insurgency after the Transition*, Asia Report No. 256, pp. 1-2, May 12, 2014; http://www.crisisgroup.org/~/media/Files/asia/south-asia/afghanistan/256-afghanistan-s-insurgency-after-the-transition.pdf.

[200] CRS Report RL30588, *Afghanistan: Post-Taliban Governance, Security, and U.S. Policy*, by Kenneth Katzman.

[201] OMB, Table S-10 in *FY2015 Mid-Session Review*, July 2014 (includes amended war request, and post-sequester funding in FY2013), http://www.whitehouse.gov/sites/default/files/omb/ budget/fy2015/assets/15msr.pdf. OMB's placeholder projections have fallen each year, mirroring policy decisions about troop levels; for example, in FY2012 President's Budget assumed a $50 billion placeholder in the outyears. See Table S-10 in OMB, *FY2011 Budget, Summary Tables*, http://www.whitehouse.gov/omb/ budget/fy2011/assets/tables.pdf.

[202] See Table 1-7 in CBO, *Update to Budget and Economic Outlook*, August 2014, http://www. cbo.gov/sites/default/files/ cbofiles/attachments/45653-OutlookUpdate_2014_Aug.pdf.

[203] OMB, Table S-10 in *FY2015 Mid-Session Review*, July 2014, http://www.whitehouse.gov/ sites/default/files/omb/budget/ fy2015/assets/15msr.pdf.

[204] OMB, *Fiscal Year 2015 Budget of the U.S. Government*, p. 59, March 4, 2014; http://www.whitehouse.gov/sites/default/files/ omb/budget/fy2015/assets/budget.pdf.

[205] For the base budget, for example, CBO's baseline reflects the statutory BCA "sequester" caps.

[206] For the baseline projections for OCO, see pp. 434 and 475 of OMB, *FY2014 Budget, Analytical Perspectives*, http://www.gpo.gov/fdsys/pkg/BUDGET-2014-PER/pdf/ BUDGET-2014-PER.pdf; for use of proposed "savings" from lower OCO costs, see Table S-2 and Table S-3 in OMB, *FY2014 Budget*, "Summary Tables," http://www.whitehouse. gov/sites/default/ files/omb/budget/fy2014/assets/tables.pdf.

[207] CBO, Letter to Congressman Ryan, Chair, House Budget Committee, "Capping War-Related Spending," February 10, 2014, http://www.cbo.gov/sites/default/files/CappingWar-RelatedSpending_RyanLtr.pdf. See also, CBO, Blog Post, "Can Proposed Reductions in Future War-Related Spending Be Used to Offset Proposed Deficit Increases in Other Areas?" February 1, 2012, http://www.cbo.gov/publication/423916.

[208] By 2017, U.S. troops could total 2,750, including 2,000 counterterrorism forces who may stay and a substantial embassy presence. Per-troop costs could total $500,000, the pre-surge level, though this cost could be lower because the United States would.no longer be maintaining bases or conducting operations except for counterterrorism.

[209] After the Iraq withdrawal, the number of troops providing in-theater support for Iraq decreased from a pre-surge level of some 34,000 to about 25,000, or by about 27%. If the same happened for OEF support, U.S. troops would decline from 31,000 (before the surge) to 18,000 by FY2019. Together with slightly lower support for OIF countries, total in-theater support would fall from 63,000 to 38,000 by FY2019.

[210] "U.S.-Afghanistan Strategic Partnership Agreement," May 2, 2012, pp. 3, 4, and 9; CRS Report RL30588, *Afghanistan: Post-* (continued...) (...continued) *Taliban Governance, Security, and U.S. Policy*, by Kenneth Katzman; White House, "Fact Sheet: Wales Summit—NATO's Changing Role in Afghanistan," http://www.whitehouse.gov/the-press-office/2014/09/04/fact-sheet-wales-summit-nato-schanging- role-afghanistan.

[211] Mark Mazzetti and Eric Schmitt, "In a Shift, Obama Extends U.S. Role in Afghan Combat," *New York* Times, November 21, 2014, http://www.nytimes.com/2014/11/22/us/politics/in-secret-obama-extends-us-role-in-afghan-combat.html?_r=0.

[212] For an analysis of the legal issues in restricting military operations, see CRS Report RL33837, *Congressional Authority to Limit U.S. Military Operations in Iraq*, by Jennifer K. Elsea, Michael John Garcia, and Thomas J. Nicola. For examples of past enacted and proposed restrictions, see CRS Report RL33803, *Congressional Restrictions on U.S. Military Operations in Vietnam, Cambodia, Laos, Somalia, and Kosovo: Funding and Non-Funding Approaches*, by Amy Belasco et al. For recent proposals to restrict military operations, see CRS Report RL33900, *FY2007 Supplemental Appropriations for Defense, Foreign Affairs, and Other Purposes*, coordinated by Stephen Daggett.

[213] See discussion and language of the Cooper-Church amendment (Sec. 7, P.L. 91-652) in CRS Report RL33803, *Congressional Restrictions on U.S. Military Operations in Vietnam, Cambodia, Laos, Somalia, and Kosovo: Funding and Non-Funding Approaches*, by Amy Belasco et al.

[214] One provision was included in both P.L. 93-52, the Continuing Appropriations Act of 1974, and P.L. 93-50, the Second Supplemental Appropriations Act of 1973, both enacted July 1, 1973; see CRS Report RL33803, *Congressional Restrictions on U.S. Military Operations in Vietnam, Cambodia, Laos, Somalia, and Kosovo: Funding and Non-Funding Approaches*, by Amy Belasco et al..

[215] See H.R. 17123, H.R. 6531, and H.R. 15628 in Table 1 and Appendix of CRS Report RL33803, *Congressional Restrictions on U.S. Military Operations in Vietnam, Cambodia, Laos, Somalia, and Kosovo: Funding and Non-Funding Approaches*, by Amy Belasco et al..

[216] CRS Report RS20775, *Congressional Use of Funding Cutoffs Since 1970 Involving U.S. Military Forces and Overseas Deployments*, by Richard F. Grimmett; CRS Report R43760, *A New Authorization for Use of Military Force Against the Islamic State: Comparison of Current Proposals in Brief*, by Matthew C. Weed; and CRS Report RL31133, *Declarations of War and Authorizations for the Use of Military Force: Historical Background and Legal Implications*, by Jennifer K. Elsea and Matthew C. Weed.

[217] *Congressional Record*, July 25, 2014, p. H6833.

[218] *Congressional Record*, June 19, 2014, p. H5538, Roll Call Vote no. 332.

[219] *Congressional Record*, June 19, 2014; p. H5528.

[220] *Congressional Record*, June 19, 2014, p. H5529, Roll Call Vote no. 328.

[221] *Congressional Record*, May 17, 2012, pp. H3011-H3014 and H3034-H3035, and Roll Call Vote no. 264.

[222] *Congressional Record*, May 25, 2011, p. H3666 and Roll Call Vote no. 364.

[223] See H.Rept. 111-522, pp. 5 and 58 and *Congressional Record*, July 1, 2010, pp. H5358-H5407.

[224] See H.Rept. 111-522, pp. 5 and 59ff and *Congressional Record*, July 1, 2010, pp. H5358-H5407.

[225] Ibid.

[226] Requirement included in *H.Rept. 111-230* to accompany the FY2010 DOD Appropriations Act (P.L. 110-3118).

[227] Letter from Steven M. Kosiak, Associate Director for Defense and Foreign Affairs, OMB, to Robert Hale, Under Secretary of Defense, Comptroller, "Revised War Funding Criteria," September 9, 2010.

[228] This breakdown is similar to the analysis, "Changes in Per-Troop Costs" but only covers FY2009-FY2015 because DOD has not provided data for the Afghan and Iraq war before then.

[229] The categories shown in **Table D-1** reflect DOD categories used in its Overview of Contingency Operations requests between FY2009 and FY2015 though DOD does not show all categories in all years; in these cases, CRS notes the categories are na or "not available" or ns, "not specified."

[230] Though most equipment rotates with units as they deploy and redeploy, some equipment remains "in-theater" for the next unit, and would be shipped home later.

[231] While some levels of "carryover" is considered desirable to provide work when orders do not materialize, the "calculated actual carryover" is expected to exceed the "allowable" carryover in both FY2014 and FY2015 for Armdepots; see *Army Working Capital Fund, Fiscal Year (FY) 2015 Budget Estimates*, March 2014, p. 58; http://asafm.army.mil/Documents/OfficeDocuments/Budget/budgetmaterials/fy15//awcf.pdf.

In: The Cost of War …
Editor: Jamie Valdez

ISBN: 978-1-63482-935-9

Chapter 2

FY2015 Funding to Counter Ebola and the Islamic State (IS)*

Susan B. Epstein, Sarah A. Lister, Amy Belasco and Don J. Jansen

Summary

In 2014, two major global threats—the Ebola outbreak in West Africa and the Islamic State (IS) in the Middle East—caused serious concern within the Obama Administration and among Members of Congress. In November 2014, the President requested a total of $11.7 billion for responding to the Ebola crisis and combatting the Islamic State.

On November 5, 2014, the President requested $6.18 billion in FY2015 emergency appropriations for Health and Human Services (HHS), the Department of State and international assistance programs, and DOD to address the Ebola crisis domestically and overseas. The funding would enhance domestic preparedness and support overseas operations to end the current epidemic and prevent the spread of Ebola and other infectious diseases. The request included $2.43 billion for Health and Human Services, $2.10 billion for the Department of State and International Programs, and $112 million for the Department of

* This is an edited, reformatted and augmented version of a Congressional Research Service publication R43807, prepared for Members and Committees of Congress, dated March 18, 2015.

Defense to advance research and technologies to control Ebola and other infectious diseases.

Appropriations requested for a new Contingency Fund (not Overseas Contingency Operations— OCO) totaling $1.54 billion under HHS and Department of State accounts were accompanied by a request for the authority to transfer these funds to any federal agency to help meet Ebola or other infectious disease-related critical needs that may suddenly arise, both domestically and overseas. In addition to the new Contingency Fund, the request also sought transfer authority for the emergency appropriations to any other federal accounts to meet the purposes specified in the request. The Administration asserted that these authorities are necessary for flexibility and a whole-of-government approach to this crisis.

On November 10, 2014, the President submitted to Congress an amended FY2015 OCO request for an additional $5.5 billion to combat IS—nearly $5 billion for DOD and $520 million for the Department of State. This brought the FY2015 OCO request to a total of $71.4 billion.

DOD's amended OCO funding request of $4.94 billion for FY2015 was for incremental U.S. military personnel expenses; fuel, supplies, and repair costs for ground, air, and sea-based operations, as well as other support; command, control, and intelligence activities, and intelligence, surveillance, and reconnaissance, and classified activities; replacement of expended munitions; building the capacity of Iraqi security forces and Kurdish and tribal forces; providing support to coalition members; and other small-scale humanitarian relief and reconstruction activities. In addition, DOD's earlier OCO request included an allocation of $500 million to train Syrian opposition forces to combat ISIS.

The Department of State's amended OCO request of $520 million was for expanding the Center for Strategic Counterterrorism Communications' messaging in key languages; helping the moderate Syrian opposition develop capacity and credibility; supporting Jordan and Lebanon's territory and borders; humanitarian support related to IS attacks in Syria and Iraq; and expanding U.S. international broadcasting to provide a platform for moderate Muslims to voice opposition to extremism.

Both the Ebola and IS requests designated budget authority as either an emergency requirement or Overseas Contingency Operations/Global War on Terrorism (OCO/GWOT). Funds designated in this manner would effectively not be subject to the discretionary spending limits established by the Budget Control Act, 2011, as amended (P.L. 112-25), and could, therefore, increase the deficit.

The conference version of the Consolidated and Continuing Appropriations Act, 2015 (P.L. 113- 235), approved the DOD Ebola request and the $5.4 billion requested to combat the Islamic State plus an unspecified increase in Department of State OCO funds that is available to counter IS. The DOD total included $1.6 billion requested for a new Iraq train-and-equip account and $500 million to train vetted Syrian opposition forces, the more controversial elements. The FY2015 National Defense Authorization Act (P.L. 113-291/H.R. 3797), signed into law on December 19, 2014, reduced the amount and limited the authorities in a new Counterterrorism Response Partnership Fund (CTPF) that could include funds to train Syrian opposition forces, as well as other partnerships.

INTRODUCTION

In the context of legislative action to fund the government through September 30, 2015, Congress considered new funding requests from the President to counter two global issues—the Ebola crisis and the Islamic State (IS). In 2014 these two threats became major concerns within the Obama Administration and among many Members of Congress. The first cases of Ebola in Guinea, West Africa were reported in March 2014 and the outbreak proceeded to spread rapidly. The IS threat quickly came to be viewed as an immediate threat to U.S. partners and allies in the Middle East region, and a concern around the world, in late summer 2014.

On November 5, 2014, the President requested FY2015 appropriations of $6.18 billion for Health and Human Services (HHS), the Department of State and international assistance programs, and the Department of Defense (DOD) to contain the Ebola crisis domestically and overseas. On November 10, 2014, the President increased the FY2015 Overseas Contingency Operations (OCO) request by $5.5 billion to combat IS.

Congressional action on both occurred within the omnibus appropriations bill (H.R. 83/P.L. 113- 235, the Consolidated and Further Continuing Appropriations Act, 2015), providing a total of more than $10.8 billion in emergency and OCO funds to address Ebola and counter the Islamic State. The President signed the full-year funding bill into law on December 16, 2014.

THE EMERGENCY REQUEST FOR THE U.S. EBOLA RESPONSE

The November 5, 2014 request of $6.18 billion was for U.S. government efforts to contain the Ebola outbreak, enhance domestic preparedness, and improve global capability to prevent the spread of other infectious diseases. Of the $4.64 billion for immediate needs, $2.43 billion was sought for HHS and $2.10 billion for the Department of State and International Programs. Additionally, DOD would receive $112 million to advance its research and technologies to end the Ebola outbreak and other infectious diseases. For flexibility, an additional $1.54 billion would be for a Contingency Fund to be available for use within HHS and State or for transfer to other agencies, as needed. The Ebola request would designate all requested budget authority as emergency requirements, so that it would effectively not be subject to the statutory discretionary spending limits established by the Budget Control Act of 2011, as amended (P.L. 112-25, BCA).[1]

Congress included $5.41 billion in its final appropriation bill: $2.77 billion for Health and Human Services, $2.53 billion for the Department of State, and $112 million for the Department of Defense. Amounts were designated as emergency spending, and transfer authority for HHS and State was also included; however, the Contingency Fund was not. Funds requested and appropriated are displayed in *Table 1*, followed by a discussion of funding for each department. Departments were required to provide the appropriations committees with detailed spending plans within 30 days of enactment, and additional reporting over time[2] (see *Table 1*).

Table 1. Emergency Funds Requested and Appropriated for Ebola and Other Infectious Diseases Amounts are U.S. dollars in millions

Agency and/or Account	Request	P.L. 113-235	Purpose(s)
FUNDING FOR IMMEDIATE NEEDS			
HHS/CDC HHS/ASPR, PHSSEF HHS/ASPR, PHSSEF, BARDA HHS, PHSSEF	1,830.0 166.0 157.0 10.0	1,771.0 576.0 157.0 ns	Various domestic and international activities in several CDC accounts. The final appropriation provided $571 million for domestic activities and $1,200 million for international activities. Domestic training, PPE, and creating more than 50 regional Ebola Treatment Centers (ETCs). Manufacture of vaccines and treatments for clinical trials. Modeling and genetic sequencing of Ebola virus. Activity not explicitly mentioned in the final appropriation, but could be included in the ASPR PHSSEF amount above.
HHS/NIH,	238.0 25.0	238.0 25.0	Clinical trials on investigational vaccines and

Agency and/or Account	Request	P.L. 113-235	Purpose(s)
NIAID HHS/FDA			treatments. Development, review, and regulation of vaccines and treatments. FDA funding is provided in the Agriculture funding division of P.L. 113-235.
HHS Total	2,426.0	2,767.0	
USAID, Operating Expenses USAID, Inspector General	19.0 5.6	19.0 5.6	Operating costs to address Ebola outbreak in West Africa. Oversight of Ebola response in West Africa.
USAID, International Disaster Assistance	1,401.0	1,436.3	Disaster assistance to address humanitarian needs for West Africa.
USAID, Global Health Programs State/USAID, Economic Support Fund State, Diplomatic, Consular Programs State, Repatriation Loans Program	340.0 211.7 35.4 1.0	312.0 711.7 36.4 ns	Expanded USAID global health security activities to control infectious diseases and limit spread of Ebola. Training and program assistance to prevent economic and government instability during Ebola crisis, including reimbursement for earlier response. Medical support and evacuation capacity, repatriation assistance, and other needs. Repatriation loans to U.S. citizens as necessary related to Ebola outbreak. Activity not specified in P.L. 113-235.
State, International Organizations and Programs	35.0	ns	Estimated U.S. contributions to UNMEER. Activity not specified in P.L. 113-235.
State, International Organizations and Programs	50.3	ns	Voluntary U.S. contributions to WHO and International Civil Aviation Organization for support to affected countries. Activity not specified in P.L. 113-235.
State, Nonproliferation, Anti-terrorism, Demining, and Related Programs	5.3	5.3	Biosafety and hazardous materials training in affected countries, efforts to mitigate the illicit acquisition of Ebola virus, and to promote biosecurity practices associated with the Ebola virus disease outbreak response efforts.
State/USAID Total	2,104.3	2,526.3	

Table 1. (Continued)

Agency and/or Account	Request	P.L. 113-235	Purpose(s)
Defense/DARPA	112.0	112.0	Developing technologies, e.g., using antibodies from survivors, and shortening vaccine development time. P.L. 113-235 specified $95 million for defense-wide research, development, testing, and evaluation, and $17 million for defense-wide procurement.
Defense Total	112.0	112.0	
Subtotal, immediate needs	4,642.4	5,405.3	
CONTINGENCY FUNDING			
HHS, contingency funds	751.0	0.0	For the HHS PHSSEF, "to prevent, prepare for, and respond to Ebola or other infectious disease domestically or internationally."
State/USAID, contingency funds	792.0	0.0	For the USAID Economic Support Fund, emergency expenses for humanitarian, economic, stabilization aid.
Subtotal, contingency funds	1,543.0	0.0	Contingency funding not provided in P.L. 113-235.
TOTAL	6,185.4	5,405.3	

Sources: White House, Office of Management and Budget (OMB), "Estimate #4–FY 2015 Emergency Appropriations Request to Enhance the U.S. Government's Response to Ebola at Home and Abroad," November 5, 2014, http://www.whitehouse.gov/omb/budget_amendments; and text and accompanying explanatory statements for P.L. 113-235.

Note: Amounts may not add due to rounding. "ns" means account details not specified.

Acronyms: ASPR is HHS Assistant Secretary for Preparedness and Response; BARDA is HHS Biomedical Advanced Research and Development Authority; CDC is HHS Centers for Disease Control and Prevention; DARPA is Defense Advanced Research Projects Agency; FDA is HHS Food and Drug Administration; NIAID is NIH National Institute of Allergy and Infectious Diseases; NIH is HHS National Institutes of Health; PHSSEF is HHS Public Health and Social Services Emergency Fund, administered by the HHS Secretary; PPE is personal protective equipment; UNMEER is United Nations Mission for Ebola Emergency Response, and WHO is World Health Organization.

Health and Human Services (HHS)

For Ebola preparedness and response activities in the Department of Health and Human Services (HHS), the President's request sought $2.426 billion for immediate needs and an additional $751 million in contingency funding. The FY2015 consolidated appropriation provided $2.767 billion for immediate needs, more than was requested, but did not provide contingency funding. Funds are intended to support both domestic and international activities. The entire appropriated amount was designated as emergency spending, as was requested. Requested and appropriated amounts presented in *Table 1* above follows:

- $1.83 billion was requested for domestic and international Ebola response activities by the Centers for Disease Control and Prevention (CDC). Domestic activities would include assistance to states to monitor travelers, and stockpiling of personal protective equipment (PPE) for hospitals. International activities would include infection control, contact tracing, laboratory surveillance, emergency operations centers, and training in affected countries in West Africa.[3] The FY2015 consolidated appropriation provided $1.77 billion to CDC for these activities.[4]
- $176 million[5] was requested, and $576 million was provided, to support domestic Ebola responses through the Public Health and Social Services Emergency Fund account (PHSSEF, a fund administered by the HHS Secretary) for the HHS Assistant Secretary for Preparedness and Response (ASPR). Funding was requested and provided (substantially above the requested level) for Hospital Preparedness Program (HPP) grants[6] to establish additional domestic Ebola Treatment Centers, and to improve readiness to detect cases of Ebola infection throughout the nation's health system including purchase of personal protective equipment (PPE) and other supplies, and training.[7] The FY2015 consolidated appropriation did not, however, endorse the Administration's plan to establish a designated Ebola Treatment Center in every state.[8]
- $157 million was requested and provided to the HHS PHSSEF for the Biomedical Advanced Research and Development Authority (BARDA) to bring Ebola vaccines and treatments developed under National Institutes of Health (NIH) and Department of Defense contracts to advanced development and manufacture for clinical trials.

- $238 million was requested and appropriated for NIH to fund clinical trials on experimental Ebola vaccines and treatments.
- $25 million was requested and appropriated for the Food and Drug Administration (FDA) for development, review, and regulation of Ebola vaccines and treatments.[9]

Per the request, all HHS funds (both for immediate needs and contingency) would be used for "purposes of preventing, preparing for, and responding to Ebola or other infectious diseases domestically or internationally."[10] The FY2015 consolidated appropriations language provided similarly broad authority to CDC and the HHS/ASPR to address Ebola and other infectious disease threats, both domestically and abroad.[11] Additional spending flexibility was provided in the appropriations language regarding renovation of private facilities, reimbursement of uninsured healthcare costs for Ebola patients treated in the United States, and other matters.[12]

The Administration requested broad authority for the HHS Secretary to transfer any appropriated funds for Ebola response within HHS or to other departments as long as funds were to be used for the stated purpose (quoted in the paragraph above). This authority would be in addition to existing transfer authorities,[13] and would require prior consultation with OMB and 10-day advance notice to congressional appropriations committees. The FY2015 consolidated appropriation did not provide such broad transfer authority, limiting CDC funds to transfers within CDC, and PHSSEF funds to transfers within HHS.

As noted, Congress did not provide the requested contingency funding for HHS. Of the amounts appropriated, amounts to CDC and the PHSSEF remain available through FY2019, amounts to NIH remain available through FY2016, and amounts to FDA remain available until expended.

Department of State and International Assistance Programs

Title IX, Division J, of the FY2015 Consolidated and Further Continuing Appropriation Act, 2015 (P.L. 113-235), provided a total of $2.5 billion but did not provide contingency funding for Ebola efforts within the Department of State and U.S. Agency for International Development (USAID) (see *Table 1*). The act also provided some transfer authority, but the funds were to be used specifically for Ebola activities. Obligating funds for Ebola requires a 15-day notification to Congress.

For Ebola preparedness and response activities conducted by USAID and the State Department, the President requested $2.89 billion. Of that amount, $2.1 billion was for immediate responses and $792 million was for a Contingency Fund.

Throughout FY2014 and FY2015, the Department of State and the U.S. Agency for International Development (USAID) had been drawing funds from International Disaster Assistance (IDA), Global Health Programs (GHP), and Food for Peace accounts to address the Ebola crisis in West Africa, as well as receiving support from DOD. $376.8 million ($64.5 million in FY2014 and $312.7 million in FY2015) of State, Foreign Operations and Related Programs (SFOPs) and Agriculture appropriations were used to fund labs for testing; medical supplies and cots; building and supporting Ebola treatment units (ETU); training and management of safe burial teams; and training health care workers.[14]

Details of the requested and appropriated amounts follow:[15]

International Disaster Assistance (IDA)—Congress provided $1,436.3 million, $35 million more than requested for IDA. The requested $1,401.0 million for IDA included $539.2 million for clinical and non-medical management of 12 ETUs; $25 million for contact tracing; $36.8 million for burial teams training and safe practices; $208.2 million for Community Care Centers; $66.9 million for outreach activities and household protections kits to promote safe behaviors; and $269.1 million to ensure an adequate supply of personal protective equipment (PPE), which includes procurement, transport, and warehousing of PPEs. An additional $190 million was for addressing the food insecurity which has been worsened by the establishment of Ebola quarantine zones in the Ebola-affected areas resulting in reduced production; loss of labor, livelihoods, and transportation services; and higher food prices. Another $16.1 million would fund increased staffing of the Disaster Assistance Response Team (DART) and USAID's Response Management Team (RMT), and support for 20 additional staff funded by USAID's Operation Expenses (OE) account.

Global Health Programs (GHP)—For GHP, Congress appropriated $312 million, $28 million below the request of $340 million. $62 million was requested for disease surveillance, laboratories, rapid response teams, and risk mitigation in the three Ebola-affected countries; and $278 million was for the Global Health Security Agenda to establish Ebola Preparedness Plans to rapidly detect and control any introduction of Ebola in currently unaffected countries in the region.

Economic Support Fund (ESF)—Congress appropriated $711.7 million for ESF, $500 million above the request of $211.7 million. Within the request, $71.7 million of ESF emergency funding was requested to address second-order impacts in Ebola-affected countries and critical innovations in responses to the epidemic. Examples include broadcasting of primary and secondary classes to school-aged students and investing in Information and Communication Technology to establish a network that is to facilitate data sharing and disease surveillance during the outbreak and that can be used in a potential future crisis. $60 million was for rebuilding nonEbola health services in Liberia, Sierra Leone, and Guinea; and $66 million was for longer-term strengthening of basic health services in the Ebola-affected countries.

Nonproliferation, Anti-terrorism, Demining, and Related Programs (NADR)—$5.3 million was requested and enacted for existing NADR expertise of securing dangerous pathogens to be used for training of local law enforcement on imposing quarantines and securing facilities that store the Ebola virus; handling and disposing of Ebola-contaminated items; and for biosecurity and related capacity building.

Diplomatic Engagement—$36.4 million was enacted rather than the $71.4 million requested for Diplomatic and Consular Programs (D&CP), U.S. Contributions to International Organizations (CIO), and Repatriation Loans. The request was to pay for evacuations of U.S. government patients, oversight of the department efforts, outreach and reporting by VOA, U.S. contributions to the U.N. Mission for Emergency Ebola Response (UNMEER), and repatriation loans to American citizens who are exposed to the virus and need to be returned to the United States using proper, but expensive, protocol.

Contingency Fund—P.L. 113-235 provided none of the requested $792 million of ESF funds as a Contingency Fund to be available until expended. This amounted to 27% of the SFOPs emergency request. The Contingency Fund was to be available for critical needs related to the Ebola outbreak and global health security. The request included broad transfer authority of these funds to other accounts in the Department of State, USAID, or other federal agencies, provided that transfers were done in consultation with the Office of Management and Budget (OMB), only for amounts designated by the President to address critical Ebola crisis needs, in addition to existing transfer authority, and with a 10-day advance notification to the House and Senate Appropriations Committees. "Notwithstanding any other provision of law" language, arguably, would have allowed these funds to be used in countries that currently are prohibited from receiving U.S. foreign aid if they meet the criteria that there is a critical need related to Ebola in that country.[16] The

Administration stated that the transfer authority and the general provisions requested would provide the flexibility and whole-of-government approach that it said was needed to address potentially rapid changes in the Ebola crisis.

Department of Defense

Within the Consolidated Appropriation (P.L. 113-235), Congress provided $112 million for DOD to support additional research on ways to treat and prevent the Ebola outbreak in West Africa.

On September 16, 2014, President Obama announced an increase in the U.S. response to the current Ebola outbreak in West Africa. Part of that included DOD requests to reprogram excess Overseas Contingency Operations (OCO) funds appropriated for FY2014 to support the Overseas Humanitarian Disaster and Civic Aid (OHDACA) account. DOD submitted two separate prior approval reprogramming requests totaling $1 billion dated September 8 and September 17 to the House and Senate Appropriations and Armed Services Committees. The committees approved the reprogramming, but with limitations requiring additional DOD action prior to use of the funds. As of November 17, 2014, the committees had approved DOD's use of up to $750 million of the reprogrammed funds for the Ebola crisis, in part as directed by USAID. The stated purposes for the reprogrammed funds include[17]

- transportation of DOD and non-DOD personnel and supplies;
- coordinating delivery of supplies from both DOD and non-DOD sources such as isolation units, personnel protective equipment (PPE), and medical supplies;
- construction of Ebola treatment units (ETU); and
- training and education in support of sanitation and mortuary affairs functions to limit the spread of the Ebola outbreak.

For FY2015, the Administration sought $112 million in emergency-designated funds for the Defense Advanced Research Project Agency (DARPA). These funds would support medical research efforts in the United States aimed at developing Ebola treatments and preventive measures. This includes new research focused on utilizing the antibodies of Ebola survivors to provide temporary immunity for infected patients until an effective vaccine can be developed and the accelerated development and testing of new Ebola vaccines and diagnostics.[18]

DARPA's Biological Technologies Office (BTO) has previously funded medical research initiatives. The Carl Levin and Howard P. "Buck" McKeon National Defense Authorization Act for Fiscal Year 2015 (P.L. 113-291) authorized appropriations in the requested amount. The Consolidated and Further Continuing Appropriations Act, 2015, appropriated the requested $112 million as an emergency requirement pursuant to section 251(b)(2)(A)(i) of the Balanced Budget and Emergency Deficit Control Act of 1985, with $17 million in the "Procurement, Defense-wide" account available until September 30, 2017, and $95 million in the "Research, Development, Test and Evaluation, Defense-Wide," to remain available until September 30, 2016.[19]

AMENDED OCO FUNDS TO COMBAT THE ISLAMIC STATE

Within the FY2015 appropriations (P.L. 113-235), Congress included $5.4 billion in OCO funds for the Department of Defense for Operation Inherent Resolve, its ongoing efforts against the Islamic State in Iraq and Syria through U.S. airstrikes and training of Iraqi and Syrian opposition forces. While the OCO request of $520 million for the Department of State specifically designated to counter the Islamic State (IS) was not provided in the appropriations act, some State Department OCO accounts were increased with broader explanatory statement language for "other assistance" or "other areas of unrest," or "extraordinary costs, including those resulting from conflict."

Earlier, on November 10, 2014, the Administration had amended its FY2015 Overseas Contingency Operations request by adding $4.94 billion for DOD and $520 million for the Department of State to support efforts to combat the Islamic State (IS). DOD's earlier OCO request in June 2014 already had included an illustrative allocation of $500 million from the $4.0 billion requested in the Counterterrorism Response Fund (CTPF) to train and equip Syrian opposition forces to fight the Islamic State. Including this allocation, DOD's request to combat the Islamic State totaled $5.4 billion.

These amendments brought the FY2015 OCO request to a government-wide total of $71.7 billion—$7.8 billion for State and $63.9 billion for DOD. This compares with $91.5 billion—$6.5 billion for State and $85.0 billion for DOD—appropriated in FY2014.[20] Budget authority designated as Overseas Contingency Operations/Global War on Terrorism (OCO/GWOT), which is how all OCO funds are designated, is effectively not subject to the statutory discretionary spending limits established by the BCA.[21]

Department of Defense

The FY2015 Consolidated and Further Continuing Appropriations Act (P.L. 113-235; H.R. 83) enacted December 16, 2015, approved a total of $5.4 billion in OCO-designated funds for DOD to combat the Islamic State. In addition to $500 million to train vetted Syrian forces and $1.6 billion to train Iraqi security forces, this total included operational funds to conduct U.S. air strikes in Syria and Iraq and support for U.S. trainers.[22] While Congress did not adjust the funds requested for air strikes and to support trainers, considerable changes were made to the Administration's requests for monies to train Iraqi and Syrian opposition forces.

As of January 30, 2015, DOD's cost of operations to counter the Islamic State, which began August 8, 2014, totaled $1.5 billion, averaging $8.4 million per day.[23] Initially, DOD financed airstrikes and the deployment of U.S. military personnel to Iraq to conduct an assessment and provide advice using OCO funds already appropriated for FY2014. Starting October 1, 2014, DOD tapped OCO-designated funds in the FY2015 Continuing Resolution (CR, H.J.Res. 124/P.L. 113-164), a practice known as "cash flowing"—relying on current funding until supplemental funding is provided later in the year (see *Table 2*).[24]

Starting October 1, 2014, incremental costs of Operation Inherent Resolve, the new Iraq and Syria operation, were being paid from funds appropriated by Congress in the FY2015 CR. Under the CR, OCO for DOD was appropriated at a rate of operations based on the $85.4 billion in OCO funds enacted in FY2014. This was $26.6 billion above the FY2015 request of $58.6 billion.

Limits on DOD's Authority to Train and Equip Iraqi and Syrian Forces

Congress approved the $500 million requested to train and equip vetted Syrian opposition forces, which was requested within a newly established Counterterrorism Partnership Response Fund (CTPF). At the same time, the final act limited the broad authorities to train and equip forces anywhere in the world proposed in the CTPF.[25]

These limitations were first included in the FY2015 CR (P.L. 113-164), in effect until December 13, 2014. In the CR, Congress provided DOD with temporary new authority to train and equip Syrian opposition forces, but only if DOD requested and the four congressional defense committees approved reprogramming of available funds.[26] The CR permitted a broad range of training and support activities and required vetting of Syrian participants. This language paralleled Section 1209 that was included the FY2015 National Defense Authorization Act (NDAA; H.R. 3979/P.L. 113-291), which required approval of requests through reprogramming and extending the authority until December 31, 2014.[27]

In addition to reducing CTPF funding from the $4.0 billion requested to $1.3 billion, Congress narrowed the authorities requested, required that DOD submit reprogramming requests specifying how the funds would be used, which would have to be approved by the four congressional defense committees, and required extensive reporting 15 days in advance of using the funds.[28]

In November 2014, the four congressional defense committees approved a DOD reprogramming request for $225 million to begin the effort to train vetted Syrian forces.[29] In a January 16, 2015, press conference, DOD said that several hundred U.S. personnel, plus an equal number of support troops, would train Syrian opposition forces starting in March 2015, with training to be completed over the next year.[30]

Congress did not change DOD's request for operational costs to conduct air strikes against IS and provide support for U.S. trainers. According to DOD budget justification materials, the $4.94 billion is for

- incremental military personnel expenses (e.g., hardship pay) for U.S. military supporting Operation Inherent Resolve (OIR);
- fuel, supplies, and repair costs for ground operations, flying hours, and steaming hours of ships in the region, as well as other support;
- command, control, and intelligence activities, and intelligence, surveillance, and reconnaissance, and classified activities;
- replacement of expended munitions (e.g., Hellfire, Maverick, Tomahawks); and
- $1.6 billion for building the capacity of Iraqi security forces and Kurdish and tribal forces, providing support to coalition members, and other small-scale humanitarian relief and reconstruction.[31]

Adding the $500 million—included as an illustrative allocation and enacted as a cap—to train and equip Syrian opposition forces brings the total

DOD amount to combat the Islamic State in FY2015 to $5.4 billion. All of these funds were designated as OCO, and hence exempt from budget caps.

Table 2. DOD's OCO Funding: FY2014 Enacted to FY2015 Enacted In Billions of Dollars of Budget Authority

Title	FY2014 Enacted (P.L. 113-76)	FY2015 Request, Feb. 2014[a]	FY2015 Request, June OCO 2014[b]	FY2015 Nov. 2014 Amendment and FY2015 Enacted[c]	Total FY2015 OCO Request	FY2015 Continuing Resolution (H.J.Res. 124/P.L. 113-164)	Total FY2015 OCO Enacted (H.R. 83/P.L. 113-235)
Military Personnel	7.97	NS	5.39	0.14	5.54	7.97	4.97
Operation and Maintenance (O&M)[d]	63.47	NS	37.43	2.32	39.78	63.47	42.56
Revolving & Mgt. Funds	0.26	NS	0.09	0.00	0.09	0.26	0.09
Procurement	6.23	NS	5.60	0.83	6.43	6.23	7.69
RDT&E	0.14	NS	0.08	0.03	0.11	0.14	0.23
Military Construction/ Family Housing	0.00	NS	0.05	[.18]	0.05	0.00	0.22
Afghanistan Security Forces Fund	4.73	NS	4.11	0.00	4.11	4.73	4.11
Iraq Train & Equip	0.00	NS	0.00	1.62	1.62	0.00	1.62
Counterterrorism Partnership Fund (CTPF)	0.00	NS	4.00	0.00	4.00	0.00	1.30
Of Which Syria Train & Equip[e]	[0]	NS	[.50]	[0]	[.50]	[.50]	[.50]
European Reassurance Initiative (ERI)	0.00	NS	0.93	0.00	0.93	0.00	0.18
Unexploded Ordnance	0.00	NS	[.25]	0.00	0.25	0.00	0.25
Other[f]	2.36	NS	0.93	0.00	0.93	2.36	1.96
Rescissions	-0.14	NS	-0.12	0.00	-0.12	-0.14	-1.24
TOTAL OCO	85.03	79.45	58.44	4.94	63.65	85.03	63.94

Sources: CRS calculations based on Congressional Record, Joint Explanatory Statement (JES) for H.R. 83, Consolidated and Further Continuing Appropriations

Act, 2015, Division C, DOD, p. H9643-H9646, and Division I, p. H. 9947. OMB, OMB, Fiscal Year 2015 Analytical Perspectives, 3-10-14; http://www.whitehouse.gov/omb/budget/ Analytical_Perspectives. Senate Appropriations Committee, S. Rept. 113-211, Department of Defense Appropriations April, 2015 to accompany H.R. 4870, July 17, 2014; Department of Defense, "Overview: Overseas Contingency Operations Budget Amendment," November 4 2014; http://comptroller.defense.gov/Portals/45/Documents/defbudget/fy2015/amendment/ FY2015_OCO_Budget_Amendment_Overview_Book.pdf. H.J. Res. 124/P.L. 113-164; H.R. 83/P.L.113-235.

[a] OMB, Table 28-1, FY2015 Analytical Perspectives; Policy Budget Authority and Outlays by Function, Category, and Program, 3-10-14; http://www.whitehouse.gov/omb/budget/Analytical_Perspectives. NS=not specified.

[b] Department of Defense, Fiscal Year 2015 Budget Amendment, Overview, Overseas Contingency Operations, June 2014; http://comptroller.defense.gov/Portals/45/Documents/defbudget/fy2015/amendment/FY2015_Budget_Request_Overview_Book_Amended.pdf.

[c] The Joint Explanatory Statement for H.R. 83/P.L. 113-235 shows no changes in the "Explanation of Project Adjustments" for each account that refer to ISIL funding, which means that Congress approved the amount requested. Table above excludes $112 million requested and enacted as emergency funds to combat Ebola.

[d] The following accounts that are part of the O&M title are shown separately in this table: ASFF, ERI, Unexploded Ordnance, Iraq Train and Equip, and CTPF.

[e] DOD included an illustrative allocation of up to $500 in the CTPF; Congress specifically included up to $500 million within CTPF in Sec. 9016.

[f] Other includes Unexploded Ordnance, "Other Defense Programs," the Afghanistan Infrastructure Fund, and a $1.0 billion congressional add for "Readiness."

The FY2015 National Defense Authorization Act (NDAA) and Train and Equip

The FY2015 NDAA (P.L. 113-291/H.R. 3979) changed DOD's requested authorities to train and equip Syrian opposition forces and to return to train Iraqi security forces.

DOD requested a $500 million allocation of funds within the Counterterrorism Partnership Response Fund (CTPF) *to train and equip Syrian opposition forces.* The FY2015 NDAA made major changes to limit DOD's authority and increase congressional oversight and set a specific $500 million cap on funds to train and equip Syrian opposition forces. The conference bill also reduced the DOD request for the CTPF from $4.0 billion to $1.3 billion.

Congress did not accept the Administration's request to permit the Secretary of Defense to waive "any other provision of law that would otherwise prohibit, restrict, limit or otherwise constrain the obligation or expenditure of [these] funds" when setting up partnerships to train and equip foreign security forces conducting counterterrorism operations.[32] Instead, Congress

- required that partnerships generally rely on already existing authorities;
- limited the geographic scope of the CTPF to Central and Africa Commands unless the Secretary of Defense determined that U.S. security was at risk;
- required that DOD submit specific requests as reprogrammings that would have to be approved by the four congressional defense committees;
- required a plan for use of the funds within 60 days of enactment and periodic reports every 60 days;
- set vetting requirements for Syrian opposition forces that would receive training and equipment; and
- limited the duration of the fund to December 2016.[33]

Instead of the blank waiver of other laws requested, the FY2015 NDAA permitted more limited waiver authority for the Secretary of Defense of acquisition and arms sales provisions, and a more general waiver for the President if determined to be vital to U.S. national security with notification to the appropriate defense committees.[34]

Although the FY2015 NDAA approved the $1.6 billion requested for a new *Iraq train-and-equip account*, it made several revisions to DOD's proposal, including sunsetting the authority on December 31, 2016, rather than September 30, 2017.

Congressional action endorsed the definition of purposes to train and equip Iraqi and other security forces in the request where DOD would

> provide assistance to military and other security forces of, or associated with, the Government of Iraq, including Kurdish and tribal security forces, with a national security mission, to counter the Islamic State in Iraq and the Levant, including the provision of equipment, supplies, services, training, facility and infrastructure repair, renovation, construction, and stipends....[35]

The act also endorsed the Administration cost-sharing provision which capped U.S. obligations capped at 60% until Iraqi, Kurdish, and tribal security forces contribute 40% of the $1.6 billion total, in cash or in-kind; at least half of the contribution was to come from the government of Iraq.[36] The FY2015 NDAA deleted the exclusion of arms sales proposed by the Administration, which permits Iraq to count those sales as contributions.[37]

Congress accepted the sharing provision proposed that required that for U.S. funds to be fully obligated, Iraqi, Kurdish, and tribal security forces would have to contribute 40% of the $1.6 billion DOD request (including in-kind contributions), with at least half of that contribution to come from the government of Iraq. Arms sales could not count toward the contribution. The conference agreement of the FY2015 NDAA deleted the exclusion of arms sales.[38]

The enacted FY2015 NDAA also set a 25% cap on obligations and expenditures that would go into effect 15 days after the Secretary of Defense and the Secretary of State submit to the appropriate congressional committees and the House and Senate leadership a specific plan identifying the forces to receive assistance, retraining, and rebuilding. The plan is to include goals, concept of operations, timelines, types of training and other assistances, roles of other partners, number and roles of U.S. military personnel, additional military support and sustainment, and other relevant details. Ninety days later, and every 30 days thereafter, the Secretary of Defense is to submit quarterly reports of any changes.[39]

Congress also agreed to the Administration's request to expand current coalition support authorities to include reimbursing Iraq for its logistical support expenses. In addition, $15 million more would be provided for "emergencies and extraordinary payments" for "confidential military purposes," typically intelligence support.[40]

Additional U.S. Military Personnel

DOD's additional request would increase U.S. troop strength in and around Iraq and Afghanistan by some 4,000 in FY2015, including troops providing training and assistance in Iraq as well as providing additional support in the region. DOD has estimated 3,100 U.S. personnel for training activities in Iraq and about 800 to train vetted Syrian opposition forces (including support personnel).[41] With approval of most of DOD's OCO request, troop strength in and around Iraq and Afghanistan would total 79,047 including 64,482 providing in-theater support (see *Table 3*). The NDAA conference report required reporting of the number of U.S. military personnel involved.

Table 3. U.S. Military Strength, FY2014-FY2015,Amended OCO

	FY2014 Enacted	FY2015 CR	FY2015 Request	FY2015 Amdt/ Enacted	Total FY2015 Req.
Afghanistan (OEF)	37,234	ns	11,661	0	11,661
Iraq (OIR)	0	ns	0	2,904	2,904
In-theater Support	61,071	ns	63,309	1,173	64,482
Total	98,305	ns	74,970	4,077	79,047

Sources: Figure 2 in Department of Defense, Fiscal Year 2015 Budget Amendment, Overview, Overseas Contingency Operations, June 2014; http://comptroller.defense.gov/Portals/45/Documents/defbudget/fy2015/amendment/FY2015_Budget_Request_Overview_Book_Amended.pdf, and DOD, Office of the Under Secretary of Defense (Comptroller) Fiscal Year (FY) 2015 Overseas Contingency Operations (OCO) Budget Amendment Update, November 2014; http://comptroller.defense.gov/Portals/45/Documents/defbudget/ fy2015/amendment/ FY15_OCO_Budget_Amendment_Update.pdf.

Notes: Figures reflect average strength.

Department of State and International Assistance Programs

Congress did not provide OCO funds within the Consolidated and Further Continuing Appropriations Act, FY2015 (P.L. 113-235), that specifically addressed the $520 million request, although it did provide additional OCO funds. Within Title VIII, Division J of the consolidated appropriations law, International Broadcasting OCO funds are for "extraordinary costs of United States international broadcasting to Afghanistan, Syria, and Iraq," and International Disaster Assistance OCO funds are for "extraordinary costs of the United States response to international disasters and crises, including those resulting from conflict." Increased ESF OCO funds were provided for the "extraordinary costs of contingency operations in Afghanistan, Pakistan, and Iraq and other assistance."[42] Comparing the FY2015 enacted with the November 10, 2014 amended request indicates an overall increase of nearly 9% for just the amended accounts. Comparing FY2015 enacted with the FY2014 actuals indicates an overall increase of 27.6%. The D&CP OCO account is the only one to decline compared with both the total FY2015 request and FY2014 actual funding levels (see *Table 4*).

For FY2015 Department of State efforts against IS, the $520 million amendment requested

- $8.6 million for D&CP to expand the Center for Strategic Counterterrorism Communications' counterterrorism messaging in key languages and increase outreach and training programs aimed at countering IS propaganda;
- $100 million for ESF to engage the moderate Syrian opposition and improve its capacity and credibility;
- $250 million for FMF to support Jordan and Lebanon's efforts to protect their national territory and maintain control over their borders;
- $65 million for PKO to increase the capacity of the moderate Syrian opposition to counter IS;
- $90 million for IDA to provide humanitarian support related to IS attacks in Syria and Iraq, including food, protection, shelter, clean water, and other supplies; and
- $6.3 million to increase VOA broadcasting in Kurdish and Turkish language services, expand Middle East Broadcasting Network's Alhurra and Radio Sawa efforts to amplify and provide a platform for moderate Muslims to voice opposition to extremism over TV, radio, and Internet platforms.

A requested amendment to the General Provisions said: *notwithstanding any other provision of law, funds appropriated under this Act may be used to provide assistance for the Syrian opposition.* If agreed to, this language would have allowed the Administration to use any FY2015 State, Foreign Operations appropriations account and either enduring or OCO funds for aid to the Syrian opposition. "The Syrian opposition" was not defined in the Administration's proposal, and U.S. officials continue to acknowledge that the opposition suffers from a lack of organization and from infighting, and includes groups whose ideologies and goals may not be compatible with U.S. long-term preferences for the region. Congress granted a more fully defined notwithstanding authority for the ESF account in the FY2014 appropriations act and outlined criteria for the use of funds and created strategy and notification requirements in relation to the authority.[43] While Congress did not provide the requested language for FY2015, it did include some limited transfer authority for the OCO funds.

Table 4. OCO:A Comparison of FY2014 Estimates vs. the FY2015 Amended Request and Enacted for Accounts to Support Combatting IS (In $ Millions)

	FY2014 actual	*Nov. 10, 2014, Amendmt.*	*Total FY2015 Request*	*Total FY2015 Enacted*	*% change FY15 enacted vs. FY15 Request*	*% change FY15 enacted vs. FY2014 actual*
D&CP	$1,391.1	$8.6	$1,562.0	$1,350.0	-13.6%	-3.0%
ESF	$1,656.2	$100.0	$1,778.4	$2,114.3	+18.9%	+27.7%
FMF	$526.2	$250.0	$862.0	$866.4	+0.5%	+64.7%
PKO	$200.0	$65.0	$180.0	$328.7	+82.6%	+64.4%
IDA	$924.2	$90.0	$725.0	$1,335.0	+84.1%	+44.4%
Int'l Broadcasting Operations	$4.4	$6.3	$6.3	$10.7	+69.8%	+143.2%
Total	$4,705.9	$519.9	$5,113.7	$6,005.1	+8.7%	+27.6%

Source: The Department of State Congressional Budget Justification, FY2015 and FY2016, the White House Amendment of June 26, 2014, and the White House Amendment of November 10, 2014.

Notes: This table presents only the OCO accounts that were amended by the President's November 10, 2014, request. In addition to these accounts, enacted USAID OCO for FY2015 increased over requested by 93.1%, FY2015 enacted INCLE OCO funds increased over requested by 11.9%, and FY2015 enacted NADR OCO funds increased over requested by $99.2 million dollars over none requested. For more detail on FY2016 State Department OCO funds, see CRS Report R43901, State, Foreign Operations, and Related Programs: FY2016 Budget Overview, by Susan B. Epstein, Marian L. Lawson, and Alex Tiersky.

Issues for Congress

Contingency Funds. P.L. 113-235 did not provide the requested contingency funds. Some in Congress had expressed concern about the request for $1.54 billion in an Ebola Contingency Fund for HHS and State. As worded in the request, the broader transfer authority, in addition to existing authority, would have allowed these funds to be transferred to any agency and among appropriation accounts, as long as the funds are used "for emergency expenses related to the humanitarian, economic, and stabilization crisis due to the Ebola outbreak." Of further note was the notwithstanding language included in the

SFOPs ESF Contingency Fund. That would have allowed these funds to be provided to countries that may currently be prohibited in law from receiving U.S. aid, or otherwise bypass other congressional restrictions or mandates.

The Administration stated that given the changing nature of the Ebola epidemic and the need to address unforeseen outbreaks before they become epidemics, HHS and State Department Contingency Funds must be accompanied by the authority giving the Administration "maximum flexibility to respond quickly," both domestically and overseas.[44] Only the funds designated by the President as critical to address the Ebola outbreak and global health security would have been obligated, according to the request, and a 10-day advance notification to House and Senate Appropriations Committees would have been required before funds could be transferred. The Administration said that structuring the Contingency Fund in this way would have supported its whole-of-government approach while allowing the Secretaries of HHS and State to oversee the allocation of the funds toward the most pressing needs.

Ebola Emergency Response Act (H.R. 5710). On November 14, 2014, Representative Christopher Smith (NJ) introduced the Ebola Emergency Response Act (H.R. 5710). It was reported out of the House Committee on Foreign Affairs on November 20, 2014, with no further action taken. It would have authorized $1.801 billion for FY2015 emergency aid for countries directly affected by an Ebola outbreak. Similar to the President's request, it included notwithstanding language and required consistency with International Disaster Assistance law within Section 491 of the Foreign Assistance Act of 1961 that would allow any country to receive U.S. aid for natural or manmade disasters and humanitarian concerns.

The legislation was an authorization of funds, not an appropriation, and also would have authorized the President to use resources from any agency on a non-reimbursable basis, subject to consent of the agency head and notwithstanding any provision of law related to limitations on the use of authorities or funding of such other agency. The bill would have required notification to the House Committees on Foreign Affairs, Energy and Commerce, Armed Services, and Appropriations, and the Senate Committees on Foreign Relations, Health, Education, Labor, and Pensions, Armed Services, and Appropriations within 15 days *after* use of this authority. A report to the above congressional committees would have been required within 6 months after the Ebola epidemic has been contained.

State Department Amended OCO for Combatting IS. Within the amended SFOPs OCO request was a General Provision notwithstanding language that would have allowed any FY2015 funding in the SFOPs appropriations act (not just OCO) to be used for combatting IS. This would have allowed both enduring and OCO funds to be used to support the Syrian opposition. While Congress did include some limited transfer authority for OCO funds, it did not agree to the notwithstanding language requested.

DOD Amended OCO for Combatting IS. H.R. 3979, the conference version of the FY2015 NDAA, continued the Continuing Resolution provision that funds training of vetted Syria opposition forces, and approved the DOD request for $1.618 billion for a new Iraq train-and-equip account. The conference also rejected the broad authorities for the CTPF requested and included additional reporting requirements for both the Iraq and Syria train-and-equip authorities.[45]

As this program is implemented, Congress may want to raise several budgetary and policy oversight issues about the funding provided:

- Will the $1.6 billion provided cover DOD's Iraq training plans and could some funding be available from other DOD OCO funds that may be larger than needed?[46]
- What are the pros and cons of the requested train-and-equip authority for Iraq for Syria, and how might Congress make adjustments during implementation if problems develop? Is the cost-sharing arrangement with Iraq practical?
- Would Congress want to define or limit the missions of U.S. troops deployed in Iraq or training Syrian forces through an Authorization for the Use of Military Force?

OCO and Emergency Spending Designations. The President's $6.18 billion request to counter Ebola designated those funds as "emergency" requirements and the $5.4 billion budget authority to counter the Islamic State as "OCO/GWOT." As enacted, this funding is exempt from statutory discretionary spending limits under the Budget Control Act.[47] The FY2016 budget and beyond may include additional funding for these missions. Congress may want to consider whether these programs are temporary or enduring requirements that would be funded in DOD's base budget.

End Notes

[1] For more information about these spending limits, see OMB, "Sequestration Update Report to the President and Congress for Fiscal year 2015," August 20, 2014, available at http://www.whitehouse.gov/sites/default/omb/assets/legislatve_reports/sequestration/sequestration_update_august2014.pdf.

[2] The Department of Health and Human Services spend plan: Ebola Emergency Funding Spend Plan, January 12, 2015; the Department of State's spend plan: Section 9004 Ebola Report and Congressional Notification U.S. Department of State and U.S. Agency for International Development, January 16, 2015.

[3] For more information, see CRS Report IF10022, The Global Health Security Agenda and International Health Regulations, by Tiaji Salaam-Blyther.

[4] Of note, requested funds are separate from charitable funds available to CDC. In 1992 Congress established the nonprofit National Foundation for the Centers for Disease Control and Prevention to aid the agency in its broad public health mission. (Public Health Service Act §399G; 42 U.S.C. 280e-11.) The CDC Foundation reported in 2014 that it had received commitments and donations of more than $43 million toward the Ebola response. Ariana Eunjung Cha, "In Ebola Fight, Private Foundations Provide Critical Financial Aid," Washington Post, November 16, 2014. See also CDC Foundation, http://www.cdcfoundation.org/.

[5] This amount includes the $10 million requested for modeling and genetic sequencing of Ebola virus. The FY2015 consolidated appropriations law did not explicitly address genetic sequencing, but this could be included in the $576 million provided through the PHSSEF for HHS/ASPR.

[6] HHS Office of the Assistant Secretary for Preparedness and Response, Hospital Preparedness Program (HPP), http://www.phe.gov/PREPAREDNESS/PLANNING/HPP/Pages/ default.aspx.

[7] On December 2, 2014, HHS announced the designation of 35 Ebola Treatment Centers in 11 states and the District of Columbia. HHS, "35 Hospitals Designated as Ebola Treatment centers," press release, December 2, 2014, http://www.hhs.gov/news. Also, the White House reiterated the funding request to continue to "build out" Ebola treatment and assessment hospitals. White House, "Update on the Ebola Response," fact sheet, December 2, 2014, http://www.whitehouse.gov/the-press-office/2014/12/02/fact-sheet-update-ebola-response.

[8] E.S., p. 110.

[9] For more information about FDA's role, see FDA, "Ebola Response Updates from FDA," http://www.fda.gov/ EmergencyPreparedness/Counterterrorism/MedicalCountermeasures/ucm410308.htm.

[10] White House, Office of Management and Budget (OMB), "Estimate #4–FY 2015 Emergency Appropriations Request to Enhance the U.S. Government's Response to Ebola at Home and Abroad," November 5, 2014, p. 8, http://www.whitehouse.gov/omb/budget_amendments. This approach is common for HHS communicable disease control programs. It recognizes that many domestic and international activities that are planned or underway to address the Ebola outbreak—such as establishing Ebola treatment centers domestically and emergency operations centers in African countries—would expand capacity for the prevention and control of other infectious diseases in the future.

[11] For now, pages 391-392 of the enrolled bill.

[12] Ibid., p. 392.

[13] See "Transfers" section of CRS Report R43304, Public Health Service Agencies: Overview and Funding.

[14] West Africa – Ebola Outbreak – Fact Sheet #1 (FY15), USAID, October 1, 2014, and West Africa – Ebola Outbreak – Fact Sheet #8 (FY2015), USAID, November 19, 2014. http://www.usaid.gov/ebola/.

[15] Emergency Request Justification, Department of State, Foreign Operations, and Related Programs, FY2015 and P.L. 113-235, Division J, Title IX.

[16] Foreign aid may be suspended or denied for a range of foreign policy and national security reasons, including support of international terrorism, human rights violations, trafficking in persons, trafficking in illicit narcotics, coercive family planning programs, denial of religious freedom, disrupting regional stability, and engaging in weapons proliferation, to name a few. The United States currently maintains robust sanctions regimes against foreign governments it has identified as supporters of acts of international terrorism (Cuba, Iran, Sudan, Syria), nuclear arms proliferators (Iran, North Korea, Syria), egregious violators of international human rights standards (Belarus, Burma, Cuba, Iran, North Korea, Russia, Syria), and those threatening regional stability (Iran, North Korea, Russia, South Sudan, Sudan, Syria).

[17] Prior Approval Reprogramming Request FY14-16 dated September 6, 2014, "September 2014 Prior Approval Request," available at http://comptroller.defense.gov/Portals/45/Documents/ execution/reprogramming/fy2014/ prior1415s/14-16_PA_September_2014_Request.pdf and Prior Approval Reprogramming Request FY14-17 dated September 16, 2014, "Additional Ebola Response" available at http://comptroller.defense.gov/Portals/ 45/ Documents/execution/reprogramming/fy2014/prior1415s/14-17_PA_Ebola_Response. pdf.

[18] "Department of Defense Research, Development, Test, and Evaluation," p. 21 of the enclosure letter from the Director of the Office of Management and Budget to the President submitting the FY2015 emergency appropriations request, November 5, 2014. See http://go.usa.gov/HPgH.

[19] See "Title X—Ebola Response and Preparedness" of Division C of P.L. 113-235.

[20] Congressional Record, "Joint Explanatory Statement, H.R. 83," p. H9646.

[21] See footnote 3.

[22] P.L. 113-235 sets a $500 million cap on funding to train and equip vetted Syrian opposition forces within the Counterterrorism Partnership Fund. The Joint Explanatory Statement for H.R. 83/P.L. 113-235 shows no changes to ISIL funding in the "Explanation of Project Adjustments" for each account, which means that Congress approved the amount requested.

[23] DOD, "Special Report, Operation Inherent Resolve, Targeted Operations Against ISIL Terrorists," visited March 6, 2015, http://www.defense.gov/home/features/2014/0814_iraq/.

[24] For example, DOD used OCO-designated FY2015 O&M, Navy and O&M, Air Force funds to conduct air strikes in Iraq and Syria because these funds finance that type of expense.

[25] DOD had requested a $500 million allocation to train and equip Syrian opposition forces within the CTPF. Congress included a specific cap of up to $500 million for that purpose within the CTPF.

[26] §149, P.L. 113-164 (H.J.Res. 124). The committees are the House and Senate Armed Services Committees and the House and Senate Appropriations Committees. The CR was extended twice—in P.L. 113-202 and P.L. 113-203 until passage of final appropriations

[27] See section below for further details.

[28] CRS Report R43727, Train and Equip Authorities for Syria: In Brief, by Christopher M. Blanchard and Amy Belasco.

[29] DOD, Reprogramming Request 15-02PA, Syria Train and Equip, November 10, 2014; http://comptroller. defense.gov/Portals/45/Documents/execution/reprogramming/fy2015/ prior1415s/15- 02_PA_Syria_Train_and_Equip.pdf. DOD, Reprogramming Request, 15-07IR, Syria Train and Equip, November 10, 2014; http://comptroller.defense.gov/Portals/ 45/Documents/execution/reprogramming/fy2015/ir1415s/15-07_IR_Syria_Train_Equip.pdf.

[30] Department of Defense, press conference with Rear Admiral John Kirby, January 16, 2015, http://www.defense.gov/ Transcripts/Transcript.aspx?TranscriptID=5573.S.

[31] DOD, Office of the Under Secretary of Defense (Comptroller) Fiscal Year (FY) 2015 Overseas Contingency Operations (OCO) Budget Amendment Update, p. 2 and p. 3, November 2014, http://comptroller.defense.gov/Portals/45/Documents/defbudget/fy2015/amendment/FY15_ OCO_Budget_Amendment_Update.pdf.

[32] Ibid., p. 12.

[33] For CTPF reduction, see Sec. 4502 in Division D, Funding Tables in H.R. 3979; these tables do not segregate the November 2014 budget amendment to counter ISIS from the earlier DOD OCO request except for the Iraq train and equip request; Text, H.R. 3979, Rules Committee print 113-58, House Amendment to the Text of S. 1847, [Showing the text of the Carl Levin and Howard P. "Buck" McKeon National Defense Authorization Act for Fiscal Year 2015.], draft conference of FY2015 NDAA; http://www.armed-services.senate.gov/imo/media/doc/CPRT-113-HPRT-RU00- S1847.pdf. See Section 1534 for conditions applying to the CTPF.

[34] Sec. 1236(j) in Ibid.

[35] Office of Management and Budget, Estimate #5—FY 2015 Budget Amendments: Department of Defense (DOD) and Department of State and Other International Programs (State/OIP) to implement the Administration's Strategy to Counter the Islamic State of Iraq and the Levant (ISIL) and update the FY 2015 Overseas Contingency Operations funding levels for both DOD and State/OIP, p. 11, 11/10/14; http://www.whitehouse.gov/sites/default/ files/omb /assets/ budget_amendments/amendment_11_10_14.pdf.

[36] Ibid., p. 12.

[37] §1236 in Rules Committee print 113-58, House amendment to the text of S. 1847, http://www.armedservices.senate.gov/imo/media/doc/CPRT-113-HPRT-RU00-S1847.pdf.

[38] §1236 in Rules Committee print 113-58, House amendment to the text of S. 1847, http://www.armedservices.senate.gov/imo/media/doc/CPRT-113-HPRT-RU00-S1847.pdf.

[39] Sec. 1236 in Ibid. "Appropriate" committees include House and Senate Armed Services and Appropriations Committees, House Foreign Affairs and Senate Foreign Relations Committees.

[40] Ibid., p. 9.

[41] Department of Defense, Press conferences with Admiral John Kirby, January 6, and January 9, 2015; http://www.defense.gov/Transcripts/Transcript.aspx?TranscriptID=5563, and http://www.defense.gov/Transcripts/ Transcript.aspx?TranscriptID=5561

[42] See Explanatory Statement for H.R. 83/P.L. 113-235, Division J, Title VIII.

[43] Section 7041(i) of Division K of the FY2014 Consolidated Appropriations Act (H.R. 3547, P.L. 113-76) significantly expanded the Administration's authority to provide nonlethal assistance in Syria for certain purposes using the Economic Support Fund (ESF) account. Such assistance had been restricted by a series of preexisting provisions of law (including some terrorism-related provisions) that required the President to assert emergency and contingency authorities to provide such assistance to the Syrian opposition and communities in Syria. The new authority made FY2014 and prior-year ESF funding available "notwithstanding any other provision of law for nonlethal assistance for programs to

address the needs of civilians affected by conflict in Syria, and for programs that seek to—(A) establish governance in Syria that is representative, inclusive, and accountable; (B) develop and implement political processes that are democratic, transparent, and adhere to the rule of law; (C) further the legitimacy of the Syrian opposition through cross-border programs; (D) develop civil society and an independent media in Syria; (E) promote economic development in Syria; (F) document, investigate, and prosecute human rights violations in Syria, including through transitional justice programs and support for nongovernmental organizations; and (G) counter extremist ideologies."

[44] Enclosed letter from the director of the Office of Management and Budget to the President submitting the FY2015 emergency appropriations request, November 5, 2014.

[45] See Sec. 1236 for Iraq train-and-equip and other sections in Title XII for expansion of current train-and-equip programs rather than the Administration's proposal; Rules Committee print 113-58, House amendment to the text of S. 1847, http://www.armed-services.senate.gov/imo/media/doc/CPRT-113-HPRT-RU00-S1847.pdf.

[46] DOD obligations for FY2014 have been slower than in the previous five years, suggesting that substantial one-year monies may expire prior to being obligated. In addition, DOD requested reprogrammings using $2.6 billion O&M, Army as a source because the withdrawals have been faster than anticipated. If less funds are needed in FY2014, and the withdrawal is ahead of schedule, the FY2015 request may also be overstated.

[47] Such designations are pursuant to §251(b)(2)(A) of the Balanced Budget and Emergency Deficit Control Act of 1985. If Congress were to consider appropriations that were designated as an emergency, a point of order against that designation that requires 60 votes to waive may be raised in the Senate. That Senate point of order does not apply to funds designated as OCO/GWOT.

INDEX

D

E

N

O

P

Q

R

S

T

U

V

W

Y